American Po' Boy En Cuba

*COMMERCIALISM & CAPATILISM CLASHING WITH
CUBA'S COMMUNISM, CULTURE, CUSTOMS, & CIVIL RIGHTS*

Practitioner's Edition

A.D. WINTERS, LLM²

Copyright © 2018 A.D. Winters, Esq. LLM²

All rights reserved.

ISBN:
978-1-7327022-1-9

All rights reserved. This book or any portion thereof may not be reproduced or used in any manner whatsoever without the express written permission of the publisher except for the use of brief quotations in a book review.

Printed in the United States of America

First Printing, 2018

Pearl Street Publishing
c/o Winters & Associates, PLLC
301 N. Main Street
22nd Floor Suite 2200
Baton Rouge, LA 70802

www.veteransdefender.com

ACKNOWLEDGMENTS

I have to start by thanking my awesome family. I honor you and cherish you. To Lula Mae Turner and Ora Dean Winters, thank you both for being my amazing mothers, who reared and birth me. B, thank you for being the most beautiful, loving, understanding, FORGIVING, and brilliant person, that I have ever met. Thanks to my children, Justen, Braden, Triniti, Farooq, and Skye for being patient and understanding of my absence during the service to the nation, the State of Louisiana, and the practice of law. To all of my siblings, thanks for the love, talks, life lessons, mentorship, and fellowship. To Erica, my sister and life-long best friend, thanks for inspiring me to pursue my academic passion irrespective of our humble beginnings. Most importantly, thanks for rapping and beat-boxing with me. To my personal mentors, Roy and Katie, thanks for putting up with and housing me and launching me into Southern University. Thanks for providing me a beacon for patterning my life. To my fraternity brethren (Masons and Kappas alike), thanks for listening to all of the Cuba thoughts and reading early drafts. To Dedrick, Deryl, Exkano, Jeff, Trevor, and Doug, thanks for believing. To all of my Professors, I'm grateful for your training me, pushing my research, and advising me on getting this book done. Specifically, Professor Donald North, thanks for being my greatest professional mentor. Your passion for service to indigent defenders and human rights moves me and challenges my best self. Your selfless sacrifice to our nation, Southern University Law Center, and devotion to family is unmatched. To Professors

Tracy Hester and Samir Foteh, University of Houston Law Center, thanks for supporting my academic growth. Thanks for the professional debates and allowing my true academic voice to shine through. Thanks for your professional support in uniquely individual ways. To Professor Matt Steffey, homeboy at Mississippi College School of Law, thanks for seeing this vision as a spark that turned into a fiery inner personal mandate. To my secretaries and legal assistants, thanks for allowing me to learn from you and take credit for your work (Ms. Stephens, Ms. Washington, Jackie, and Sherrie). To my comrades in the Armed Forces and fellow Veterans, thanks for allowing me to tag along for more than two decades and I'm grateful for your service. To the amazingly intellectual and cultured Cuban people that took time out of their busy lives to engage me, thank you for educating me and proudly revealing your culture and truths, with spirited debates and illuminations. Viva La Cuba Libre!

Table of Contents

CHAPTER 1: SO WHAT, NOW WHAT? 11

1.0 Now that the Obama Administration Has Engaged Cuba, So What, Now What? 12

1.1 Introduction 12

1.2 The History of Cuba 14

1.2.1 The U.S. Cuban Relations 17

1.2.2 Spanish American War 17

1.2.3 PLATT AMENDMENT..19

1.3 Cold War Era: Cuban Revolution 23

1.3.1 The Granma 82 24

1.3.2 Revolución Cubana 26

1.4 The Making of the Embargo. 27

1.4.1 The Taking..30

1.5. American Acts of Aggression Toward Cuba (Terrorism?).........32

1.5.1 BAY OF PIGS 34

1.5.2 Operation Mongoose 35

1.5.3 Cuban Missile Crisis 36

1.5.4 Cuban Americans Influence on Foreign Policy.......................37

1.5.5 Cuban-American National Foundation 39

1.5.6 Immigration Crisis..41

1.5.7 The Initial Codification of the Embargo 41

1.6. The Changing Tide of Americans of non-Cuban Descent 42

1.7. Brothers to the Rescue...43

1.8. Extraterritorial Application 44

1.8.1 Why a BIT can help a bit? From Gunboat Diplomacy to Bilateral Investment Treaties 46

1.8.2 BITs Historically 46

1.8.3 BITs Protection from an International Perspective 48

1.9. Cuba's Foreign Investment Protections 54

1.9.1 Cuba's Expropriation Model: 54

1.9.2 Cuba's take on Foreign Investments and BITs 58

1.9.3 The BIT from the Cuban Perspective 59

1.9.4 Domestic Protection Offered to the Foreign Investors 61

1.9.5 Cuban BIT Litigation 64

1.10. U.S.- Cuban Relations 2014 and Beyond 69

1.10.1 So What for Texas? 71

1.10.1.1 So What For Louisiana? 75

1.10.2 Modern U.S. Cuba Relations 76

1.10.2.1 So What For the Intellectual Property (Trademark) of American Business? 77

1.10.2.2 So What For Trademarks? In Use 78

1.10.3 What were some underlying causes for the Obama Administration's Policy Shift? 79

1.10.4 Obama's Actions 82

1.10.5 Under What Authority, Does Obama (and now Trump) Enact Easing Regulations? 85

1.11. Cuba's Economic Lessons Learned 89

1.11.1 The Special Period and Beyond 89

1.11.2 Take It or Leave It Valuation? 95

1.12. The BIT from the U.S. Perspective 96

1.12.1 U.S. Federal Arbitration Agreement 96

1.12.2 Texas State Arbitration Agreement... 97

1.12.3 U.S. BIT Litigation.. 100

1.13. Best Practices in BIT Establishment 102

1.14. Conclusion 103

CHAPTER 2: ALL AROUND THE WORLD, SAME SONG! 107

2.0 INTRODUCTION 108

2.1 Equal Protection 110

2.2 Equality in the U.S. 111

2.21 Latin American Equality 117

2.22 Castro Equality 119

2.3 Religious Freedom 123

2.31 Latin American Region's Religiosity 126

2.32 Castro's Losing and Regaining His Religion 128

2.4 A Rainbow Coalition 133

2.41 LGBTI Development in Latin America 133

2.42 U.S. LGBTI Rights... 135

2.43 Cuba's Progress 139

Chapter 3: DEFINING CORPORATE COMPLIANCE WITH A REKINDLED U.S. & CUBA RELATIONSHIP 143

3.1   Executive Summary 144

3.2	Thesis:	144
3.3	Background.	145
3.4	Regulatory Framework.	148
3.4A.	Cuban Assets Control Regulations	148
3.4A1.	Previous Presidential Administrations.	149
3.4A2.	Obama Regulations	152
3.4A3.	Candidate Trump	156
3.4A4.	President Trump's First One Hundred Days and Beyond	157
3.4A5.	Miguel's at the Helm	158
3.4B.	External Influences	159
3.4B1.	Regional and Hemispheric Neighbors	159
3.4B2.	United Nations' Concerns	159
3.4B3.	Castro-out	160
3.4B4.	Castro-in	160
3.5.	Cuba remains a viable option for foreign companies to sustain a profit despite the compliance restraints, regulatory framework, and socio-economic challenges.	161
3.5A.	Cuban & American citizens support engagement policies.	161
3.5A1.	Common Myths from the Cuban Perspective	163
	Myth: The Castro's are creating a family dynasty like North Korea.	165
3.5A2.	Myths from an American Perspective	166

Myth: The United States has gotten nothing in return for

concessions made to Cuba. 166

3.5A2.a. Cuban Americans Attitudes Shifted. 168

3.5A2.b. Polls Don't Lie. 169

3.5A2.c. Travel Has Increased. 170

3.5A2.d. The Trump Effect on Traveling to Cuba. 173

3.5A2.d. So What, Can You Travel to Cuba? 174

3.5B. Advantages of the Cuban Market 175

3.5B.1. The Trump Effect on Cuban Business' Dreams 182

3.5C. Voluminous Regulatory Requirements, Restrictions, and Risks Presents Pitfalls and Potential. 182

3.5C1. Disadvantages and Pitfalls 188

3.5C2. Extreme Bipartisanship 199

3.5C3. Personal Risks 201

3.5C4. The Carters En Cuba (Jay-Z and Beyoncé) 202

3.5C5. Business Risks 206

3.5D. Comprehensive Compliance Program 208

3.5D1. Compliance HSE Management 209

3.5D2. Bayer Bears an Exemplary Compliance Program 210

3.6. Foreign and American businesses currently operating in Cuba are finding success. 213

3.6A. International Community 213

3.6A.1. Canadian Sherritt International 213

3.6A.2. China 214

3.6A.3. United Kingdom 217

3.6B.   Most Americans won't be able to do business immediately. 218

3.6C.   Proof of Principles... 220

3.6C.1.   Tech 220

3.6C.2.   Charcoal 222

3.7.   Cuba has limited capacity to absorb the American demand. 224

3.8.   Forecast and Conclusion 226

Predictions and Conclusion 226

Conclusion... 233

CHAPTER 4: QUICK GUIDE TO VISITING CUBA 234

4.0   Look Before You Leap to the Pearl of the Caribbean 235

4.1 On Day 1 – Debarkation into Cuba... 236

4.2 On Day 2: - Exploring the city of Havana and its rich history 237

4.3 On Day 3: – Ernest Hemingway's house 240

4.4 On Day 4: – Community services, dance................................ 241

4.5 On Day 5: – Education and history 242

4.6 Day 6 – Community services 243

4.7 Day 7: – Arts, Domestic and International Law in Cuba 244

CHAPTER 5: PHOTO COLLAGE FROM THE PEARL OF THE CARRIBEAN 246

CHAPTER 1: SO WHAT, NOW WHAT?

Now that the Obama Administration Has Engaged Cuba, So What, Now What?

Abstract

Bottom line, both the governments and their citizens, whether juridical or natural, in the United States and Cuba need to exhibit patience, understanding, respect, and continued engagement.

A.D. Winters, Esq. LLM[2]

1.0 Now that the Obama Administration Has Engaged Cuba, So What, Now What?

1.1 Introduction

On December 17, 2014 or as the Cubans call it ("17 D")[1] *Diez y siete Deciembre*, President Barack Obama and Cuban President Raul Castro announced their collective lofty intentions to restore diplomatic relations with Cuba and to ease the U.S. economic sanctions against the neighboring island. This section will examine many themes that brought the two nations to this point to include but not limited to Cuba's History, America and Cuba's historical diplomacy, Cuban's spirit of independence and an initial constitution. Additionally, the unit will examine the Platt amendment and its impact on Cuban's independent mindset. After that, the discussion moves to Fidel Castro-led revolution and his subsequent ascension to power.

The book then shifts focus to the Castro years and the expropriation of assets. Here, the focus moves toward evaluating the embargo and the great exodus of Cuban Americans to South Florida. That is followed by an analysis of the Cold War relationship between Cuba and the former Soviet Union and how this relationship nearly

---

[1] Feinberg, R. E. (2016). Open for business: Building the New Cuban Economy. Washington, D.C.: Brookings Institution Press.

brought the world to nuclear war.

The book then concentrates on U.S. foreign policy development as it relates to Cuba from President Ronald Reagan to President Obama and their respective Congressional and special interest influences. Here, the discussion evaluates whether the U.S. became a state that sponsored terrorism or used terroristic activities as a defense mechanism against Cuba, its Soviet benefactors, and communism.

Then, the book will take a deep-dive exploration of the embargo in the context of globalization with international influences and tools like bi-lateral investment treaties ("BITs") and multilateral trade agreements. This requires an exploration of each countries' national model contract; some of the current BITs; and trade agreements that each nation is signatory. This necessitates a deep dive into the two nations' attitude toward foreign investments; settling disputes internationally; and recent arbitral litigation to which each have been involved. This portion of the book analyzes the environment for foreign investment risks for a foreign investment in Cuba; potential settlement of old certified claims; current dispute settlements against each Cuba and whether Cuba paid. The book then illustrates some best practices that current BITs offers and enforcement under the New York and Washington Conventions.

Additionally, the book evaluates the two nations' motivation to normalize relation. Why would Cuba want the U.S. foreign investments? Have other foreign investments flourished in Cuba? What are some challenges that other foreign investments have encountered in Cuba? Finally, the book will evaluate the blueprint to a path forward to a bi-lateral investment treaty between the U.S. and Cuba.

1.2 The History of Cuba

Cuba is a relatively young nation, just under 120 years, since she achieved her independence from Spain's imperialism.[2] The island was originally inhabited by three separate indigenous peoples. These first nations were the *Ciboney*, the *Tainos*, and the *Guanajatabeyes*, who all apparently subsisted mainly on fishing and agriculture.[3] Even as far back as then these tribes figured out how to coexist albeit on fragile terms.

The Tainos were the largest of the original Cubans tribes, who had had thrived in aquaculture and skilled in weaving to build nets for fishing and hammocks for sleeping. Many consider this group to be the creators of

---

[2] Gonzalez, E. (2007). Cuban exiles on the trade embargo: Interviews. Jefferson, NC: McFarland. ("Cuban Exiles") p. 13
[3] Cuban Exiles... p. 13.

the modern-day hammocks. The Tainos further distinguished themselves by their use of tobacco in a context, and their belief in a supernatural being and life after death.[4]

The island was "discovered" by Columbus on October 28, 1492, and the first nations encountered Europeans for the first time. After several name changes, Cuba finally stuck, which most likely came from the Spaniards who realized that Cuba was strategically important and referred to as la Perla del Caribe, i.e., the Pearl of the Caribbean.[5]" Diego Velasquez, a Spanish soldier, established the first European settlement in Cuba in 1511 to support as a Spanish logistics hub and power projection platform for forward exploration and empire building into Florida, Mexico, and beyond.

In the mid-18th century, Spain decided that Cuba would be the Spanish crown's only sugar producer resulting in the proliferation of plantations of sweet cane throughout the island. This white gold expansion came on the backs of African slaves and at the overplanting of the soil. So in 1791, after the Haitian slaves stop using their machetes to cut sugar cane and began beheading their masters, Cuba was catapulted to the world's sugar

---

[4] Cuban Exiles... p. 13
[5] Cuban Exiles... p. 13.

capital.[6]

After Spain lost most of its empire in Latin America during the first quarter of the nineteenth century, Cuba became its most valuable colony, the source of wealth from sugar, tobacco, and minerals, produced largely by slaves.[7] Efforts to acquire Cuba by purchase were made informally after the United States purchased Florida in 1819 but were ignored. From 1830-40s multiple Cuban revolts which were frequently quelled in a brutal manner.

A formal effort in 1853 occurred in the wake of President Pierce's inaugural address in which he suggested further territorial purchases. Secretary of State William L. Marcy offered to purchase Cuba for US$130,000,000.[8] In 1854, the United States had sought to annex Cuba by purchase or other means as a slaveholding outpost from which U.S. slaveholding could be protected, but Northern Abolitionists would never agree to such an expansion of slavery. By that time, the Cuban economy based on sugar, was more closely connected to the United States than to Spain.[9]

---

[6] Ospina, H. C. (2002) Bacardi: The Hidden War trans. Stephen Wilkinson. London: Pluto Press. p.1. ("Bacardi")
[7] Sweeney, J. (n.d.). Guantanamo and U.S. Law. Fordham International Law Journal, 30(3), 673. ("Sweeney")
[8] Sweeney... p. 674.
[9] Sweeney... p. 674.

1.2.1 The U.S. Cuban Relations

The United States and Cuba share a complicated and closely connected history.[10] As far back as 1884, while Cuba was still under Spanish rule, the U.S. and Spain signed a commercial agreement for the improvement of mercantile relations between the U.S. and the islands of Cuba and Puerto Rico by removing tariffs and extra duty ad valorem taxes.[11]

1.2.2 Spanish American War

After the first failed Cuban run at independence in the Ten Years War,[12] the Cubans desire and thirst for freedom was not quenched. Cuban's second attempt at independence was from 1895-1898, known as the "Little War." Spain's colonial policy had been described as both "incompetent and tyrannical," especially in the 1895-1897 uprising when General Valeriano Weyler (called "the Butcher" in the U.S. press) introduced concentration camps in which thousands of Cubans died of disease and starvation.[13]

Another example of Cuban-American relations came

---

[10] Haney, P. J., & Vanderbush, W. (2005). The Cuban embargo: The domestic politics of an American foreign policy. Pittsburgh, PA: University of Pittsburgh Press. ("Cuban Embargo") p. 11.
[11] Commercial Relations With Respect To Cuba and Puerto Rico:. (1884). Retrieved November 25, 2016, from http://www.loc.gov/law
[12] 1868-1878
[13] Thomas, H. (1971). Cuba: The pursuit of freedom (2nd ed.). New York: Harper & Row. at 316-38.

during the Spanish American War, which was a conflict fought between Spain, Cuba, Puerto Rico, Philippines and the United States from April 21, 1898 to August 13, 1898 with the main issue being Cuba's independence. The U.S. was catapulted into the war after the battleship Maine was destroyed, which was allegedly sent to evacuate Americans trapped on the island. Spain likely presumed this was "Gunboat Diplomacy,"[14] in light of the U.S.' well-known desires for acquiring Cuba. The Maine exploded and sank in Havana harbor killing 266 out of the 355 sailors on board and set off a rancorous call to war with Spain by several powerful newspaper editors. President McKinley took action on April 11 by asking Congress for forcible intervention in Cuba, and Congress responded on April 20, 1898 with a Joint Resolution authorizing military force against Spain.[15]

On May 18, 1898, Congress authorized Act 345, which the U.S. provided assistance to the inhabitants of Cuba, and arms, munitions, and military stores to the people of the Island of Cuba, and for other purposes. The 55th U.S. Congress enacted Chapter 345, which allowed the

---

[14] Gunboat diplomacy, which refers to the pursuit of foreign policy objectives with the aid of conspicuous displays of naval power—implying or constituting a direct threat of warfare, should terms not be agreeable to the superior force, is antiquated and dangerous. Distinguishable is "Defense Diplomacy," which is understood to be the peaceful application of resources from across the spectrum of defense, to achieve positive outcomes in the development of bilateral and multilateral relationships. The U.S. likely used one of these during the Platt Amendment era with Cuba.

[15] Sweeney... p. 674.

U.S. military to arm the Cuban people.[16] The war was over in about ten weeks later, and concluded by the Treaty of Paris, whereby Spain relinquished all claim of sovereignty over Cuba and transferred Cuba to the United States.[17] Cuba became a U.S. protectorate in 1901.

1.2.3 PLATT AMENDMENT

The first Cuban Constitution included an addition imposed by the U.S. Congress called the Platt Amendment which recognized the right of the U.S. to intervene in Cuban internal affairs; limited the right of the Cuban government to sign treaties or obtain loans from abroad, and gave the U.S. land rights and granted the U.S. a naval base.[18] The Platt amendment, which was

---

[16] **Sec. 1. That while serving in Cuba of during the existing war, officers of the Army of the United States exercising separate commands may, by special order, cause subsistence, medical, and quartermaster's supplies to be issued to, and other aid rendered to, inhabitants of the Island of Cuba who are destitute and in imminent danger of perishing unless they receive the same.**
Sec. 2. That the President, and general officers commanding troops in Cuba, are hereby authorized to furnish to the Cuban people such arms, ammunition, equipment, and military stores and supplies as they may require in order to increase their effective fighting force in the existing war against Spain.

[17] Perez, Y. R. (2016) The Development of the Cuba-United. States Relationship. International Law Quarterly, 32(3), 8. ("Perez")

[18] Bacardi... p. 5. This book raises fundamental issues about the relationship between a multinational corporations, imperialist politics, about the instrumental use by the state of private corporations to serve as a state directed terrorism. In this book Ospina investigates whether the Bacardi company, who left Cuba just before the Castro regime came into power, has been instrumental in supporting an anticastrista movement and even terrorist activities inside Cuba. The author is

named after U.S. Senator Orville Platt and drafted in large part by War Secretary Elihu Root, laid down eight conditions to which Cuba had to agree before U.S. forces would withdraw and begin the transfer of Cuba's sovereignty.[19]

Once, these boxes were checked,[20] U.S. law directed the

---

skeptical of Bacardi success since the early years, and questions how Bacardi operated with the Cosa Nostra during the prohibition period to initiate the "rum route" between Cuba, Jamaica, and New Orleans. He inquires, "How did Bacardi sell 1 million bottles of Rum in the U.S. in the first year after prohibition, especially since the U.S. market had been closed for 14 years. Ospina and other critics view this as putting profits over patriotism. Cuban economist Jacinto Torras that Bacardi's (originally a Santiago, Cuba company) creating distribution and logistics nodes in other countries was deeply harmful to the Cuban economy.

[19] In the Relations with Cuba, a treaty signed at Havana May 22, 1903, 33 Stat. 2248; Treaty Series 437:

- [20] "I. That the government of Cuba shall never enter into any treaty or other compact with any foreign power or powers which will impair or tend to impair the independence of Cuba nor in any manner authorize or permit any foreign power or powers to obtain by colonization or for military or naval purposes or otherwise, lodgment in or control over any portion of said island."
- "II. That said government shall not assume or contract any public debt, to pay the interest upon which, and to make reasonable sinking fund provision for the ultimate discharge of which, the ordinary revenues of the island, after defraying the current expenses of government shall be inadequate."
- "III. That the government of Cuba consents that the United States may exercise the right to intervene for the preservation of the Cuban independence, the maintenance of a government adequate for the protection of life, property, and individual liberty, and for discharging the obligations with respect to Cuba imposed by the treaty of Paris on the United States, now to be assumed and undertaken by the government of Cuba."
- "IV. That all Acts of the United States in Cuba during its military occupancy thereof are ratified and validated, and all lawful rights acquired thereunder shall be maintained and protected."

President to cede control of Cuba (the eighth provision) to its government only when the Cuban government had endorsed the first seven provisions established in U.S. law by the Platt Amendment of March 1901. The 1903 Treaty of Relations noted that Cuba's Constitutional Convention had, on June 12, 1901, added the Platt Amendment provisions to its constitution on February 21, 1901. Those provisions, among other things, restricted the independence of the Cuban government and gave the U.S. the right to oversee and at times interfere in Cuban affairs. The Cuban government had taken power and the U.S. withdrawn its forces as of May 20, 1902.

The final provision of the Platt Amendment required that its provisions be adopted by treaty as well. The

---

- "V. That the government of Cuba will execute, and as far as necessary extend, the plans already devised or other plans to be mutually agreed upon, for the sanitation of the cities of the island, to the end that a recurrence of epidemic and infectious diseases may be prevented thereby assuring protection to the people and commerce of Cuba, as well as to the commerce of the southern ports of the United States and the people residing therein."
- "VI. That the Isle of Pines shall be omitted from the proposed constitutional boundaries of Cuba, the title thereto being left to future adjustment by treaty."
- "VII. That to enable the United States to maintain the independence of Cuba, and to protect the people thereof, as well as for its own defense, the government of Cuba will sell or lease to the United States lands necessary for coaling or naval stations at certain specified points to be agreed upon with the President of the United States."
- "VIII. That by way of further assurance the government of Cuba will embody the forgoing provisions in a permanent treaty with the United States."

Treaty of Relations, signed in May 1903, accomplished that.

The 1903 Treaty of Relations was superseded by the 1934 Treaty of Relations, which abrogated in large measure the 1903 treaty while affirming the U.S. right to lease land for a naval station and continuing to hold the U.S. blameless for actions taken before the establishment of the Republic of Cuba in 1902.

The treaty fell short of the original desires of both the United States government and its historical ambition of annexation of Cuba,[21] and the post Spanish-American War aim of leasing four strategically favorable port for naval bases located in Guantánamo Bay, Bahia Honda, Cienfuegos, and Nipe Bay.[22] In opposition, Cubans, evident through the generations of revolts and rebellions, were historically desirous of self-rule, and post-Platt, the government of Cuba viewed Guantanamo Naval base as a constant affront to its sovereignty, taken under duress and maintained under the threat of atomic

---

[21] Franklin, J. (2016). Cuba and the U.S. Empire: A Chronological History. New York: Monthly Review Press. In a letter to the U.S. Minister to Spain Hugh Nelson, Secretary of State John Quincy Adams described the likelihood of U.S. "annexation of Cuba" within half a century despite obstacles: "But there are laws of political as well as of physical gravitation; and if an apple severed by the tempest from its native tree cannot choose but fall to the ground, Cuba, forcibly disjoined from its own unnatural connection with Spain, and incapable of self-support, can gravitate only towards the North American Union, which by the same law of nature cannot cast her off from its bosom."

[22] Treaty of Relations. www.wikipedia.org

force.

A series of trade agreements and sugar acts followed the Platt Amendment and gave Cuban producers favorable access to the U.S. market, but these agreements also tied the Cuban economy to this single commodity. This gave the U.S. incredible leverage over the island neighbor.[23] During this period Cuba had an absolute dependence on the U.S. economy and when the Great Depression began in October 1929, the Cuban economy nearly went into an abyss. The price of sugar fell to less than 1 cent per pound, and Cuba was left toiling with the worst unemployment in the world.[24] This Platt Amendment was ended by President Franklin Roosevelt and abrogated by treaty in June 9, 1934.

1.3 Cold War Era: Cuban Revolution

The Cuban government went through a world-wind of instability in governance with no peaceful transition of power. After the Cuban economy sunk in the 1930s President Machado was sacked and sent into exile by a general uprising in 1933 supported by the Cuban army. Shortly after, his successor Miguel Mariano Gomez was impeached.[25] Then, Federico Bru, former head of the army, was installed as president to institute a series of

---

[23] Cuban Embargo… p. 13.
[24] Bacardi… p. 7.
[25] Cuban Exiles… pp. 16-17.

social and economic reform. By 1940 Fulgencio Batista was at the helm with the propagation of a new constitution. After WWII, Carlos Prio Socaras, a former cabinet member was elected to lead Cuba in 1948. Batista, supported by the Cuban army, returned in 1952 with what amounted to a coup de tat and instituted a dictatorship disbanding the Congress and suspending the constitution promising free elections.[26] The only significant opposition during this second reign of Batista was in 1953 by Fidel Castro, a young Cuban lawyer in Oriente, who Batista crushed. Batista easily won reelection and was installed as President in 1955 and had fostered a favorable relationship between Cuba and the United States.[27]

1.3.1 The Granma 82

Castro was exiled but returned reorganized using guerilla tactics with 82 or so men and garnered the public support and trust.[28] Not your ordinary run of the mill revolt, the revolution began in July 1953. Initially, like Castro's presidential opposition to Batista, the initial revolt was disastrous. Consider the 82 brave rebels sailing the *Granma* sailboat that was easily quashed by Batista's Cuban Air Force. Of the small fraction of this force that survived and regrouped in the Sierra Maestra

---

[26] Cuban Exiles… p. 17.
[27] Perez… p. 8.
[28] Cuban Exiles on the Trade Embargo.pg 17.

mountain range, Fidel and Raúl Castro, the Argentine born Warrior Ernesto 'Che' Guevara, and Camilo Cienfuegos were the core revolutionary leaders. While these leaders and revolutionaries were setting up camp in the Sierras, "Civic Resistance" groups were formulating in the cities, conducting shaping operations and putting pressure on the Batista regime. Perhaps inspired by Fidel ('a lawyer') and Che ('a doctor'), many middle-class and professional persons flocked toward the movement. The Castro led revolution began to swell until he called for a general revolt in March 1958 until Batista resigned and fled on January 1, 1959.

While in the mountains, the guerrilla forces attracted hundreds of Cuban volunteers and won several battles against the Cuban Army. During the fighting, Che was reportedly shot in the neck and chest, but continued to give first-aid to his fellow wounded guerrillas. The charismatic Che learned to master the media and turn its desire for first in reporting on its head. He founded *Radio Rebelde*, which was recognized as "the voice of the Sierra Maestra, transmitting for all Cuba."[29] The station provided first-hand reports on the battles against Batista's Army and denounced the dictator's atrocities including the harsh instruments of torture and killing of

---

[29] Some of the first words uttered on Radio Rebelde by Capt. Luis Orlando Rodriguez, Station Director.

20,000 people between 1952-1959.

1.3.2 Revolución Cubana

The Cuban Revolution continued sporadically until the rebels finally ousted Batista on 1 January 1959, replacing his government with a revolutionary socialist state. In defeat, Batista fled for the Dominican Republic, as the Movement's forces marched into Havana.

The *Revolución Cubana* continued through July 26, 1959 and is celebrated in Cuba as the *Day of the Revolution (similar to the 4th of July)*. The *26 De Julio Movement's* ultimate reformation yielded the Communist Party in October 1965. The revolution is still celebrated more than ever in present day Havana, as A.D. Winters observed the celebratory environment in July 2018.

The revolution produced powerful domestic and international ramifications. In the immediate aftermath of the revolution, Castro's government began a program of nationalization and political consolidation that transformed Cuba's economy and civil society. Some businesses were extremely weary of the self-proclaimed Cuban "people's savior's" revolution, so much so that longtime Cuban enterprise, Bacardi Rum Company left.[30] Another telling example of the defeat of Batista's ideals and vision of Havana as Latin America's premier tourist

---

[30] Bacardi…p. 20.

destination was the taking of Habana Hilton. Conrad Hilton's company developed the largest and tallest hotel on the island. Castro and his revolutionary cohorts converted the hotel into its provisional headquarters and command center. *Habana Libre* (Free Habana) proudly displays an illuminating photographic depiction of this story in its strikingly modern lobby.

In particular, the revolutionary movement transformed Cuba's relationship with the United States. The two neighbors' diplomacy dwindled quickly. From the inception of the new government, President Eisenhower recognized the Castro government on January 7, 1959[31] even before Castro was sworn in as the premier in February 1959. Then in 1961, the U.S. broke diplomatic relations with Cuba.

1.4 The Making of the Embargo.

Even though the U.S. embargo of Cuba began under President Eisenhower in 1960, the embargo was steadily tightened until it was codified into the LIBERTAD Act of 1996, more commonly known as the "Helms-Burton" act named for the legislation's sponsors. The embargo has several components: travel restrictions, restrictions on goods and services, bans on business investments, constraints on immigration, journalism and scholarly

---

[31] Cuban Embargo…p. 13.

limitations, caps on financial support sent to family members in Cuba.

Pinpointing a precise date on the origins of the embargo, which is referred to as a blockade in Cuba, is subjective.[32] In October 1960, Eisenhower prohibited U.S. oil refineries in Cuba from refining Soviet crude oil, drastically cut the Cuban sugar quota, and imposed an economic embargo on all trade with Cuba except food and medicine.[33] The purpose[34] was to reduce Cuban-American trade from $1 billion to about $100 million, and further reduce U.S. foreign direct investment into Cuba to zero. The embargo's application became increasingly restrictive with economic measures against Cuba from 1960-1962.

Even though the embargo started unilaterally, its grasp was felt through a multinational approach. For instance, the U.S. passed two substantive legislative additions were Food for Peace and Country Group Z. The Food for Freedom bill was a 1966 $3.3 Billion piece of legislation that prohibited food aid to any country engaged in trade with Cuba and North Vietnam. When India, which was scheduled to receive 11 million tons of U.S. grain,

---

[32] Kaplowitz, D. R. (1998). Anatomy of a failed embargo: U.S. sanctions against Cuba. Boulder: Lynne Rienner. ("Anatomy") p. 72.
[33] Cuban Embargo… p. 15.
[34] Cuban Exiles…p 6. The main objective of the trade embargo is to subdue opposing Armies and or political regimes that control those armies by cutting off all possible means of supplies.

operated outside the scope of the legislation by selling Cuba $4 million in jute to Cuba. The U.S. reduced India's grain allotment to 2 million tons and agreed to 3 million more tons in exchange for India agreeing not to expand its trade with Cuba.[35]

As to the Country Group Z legislation, it placed Cuba in country group Z, which is the most restrictive. This category meant prohibition of re-exports from third countries of U.S. origin with Cuba. Moreover, under the U.S. leadership, the Organization of American States expelled Cuba, broke diplomatic relations with the island, and adopted economic sanctions as well.[36]

As laid out in the book, "THE CUBAN EMBARGO: The Domestic Politics of An American Foreign Policy,[37] this tightening came about due to developments occurring under the Castro regime.[38] During the first month in power, the revolutionary government conducted a number and trials and executions of members of former Cuban President Batista's regime.[39] This was commonly known as *El Paredon*, which is Spanish for the stucco

---

[35] Anatomy...p. 72.
[36] Anatomy... p. 76.
[37] Cuban Embargo...p. 3. The goal of the book is to examine the changing politics of U.S. policy toward Cuba and the dynamics that drive policy evolving over time. The Cuban American National Foundation (CANF) initial stance during the Regan era compared now is ironic. Initially, CANF wanted to strengthen the embargo
[38] Cuban Embargo...p. 13.
[39] Cuban Embargo...p. 13.

covered masonry walls that generally surrounded a property. Under Castro, the wall took on a more sinister meaning in that his revolutionaries would force their blind-folded opposition, real or imagined, along the wall and summarily execute them.[40] One of the most revile examples of these killings was the televised firing squad execution of Colonel Cornelio Rojas, the former Chief of Police of Santa Clara. This fear tactic reverberated throughout the country.

As the international community condemned such trials and summary executions as Kangaroo courts, Castro and Che, (now head of the Revolutionary Court) launched Revolution TV trials in sort of a Roman Circus way. Hosted before 17,000 citizens in a sporting venue, the accused were pointed out and ridiculed before sentencing and summary executions.

1.4.1 The Taking

In addition to the executions and intimidation came the taking, expropriation, and nationalization. Castro announced that he would expropriate over a thousand acres of farmlands.[41] Castro, the alleged savior of his "beloved isle" nationalized industries.[42] Castro expropriated properties, businesses, and homes

---

[40] Cuban Exiles... p. 19.
[41] Cuban Embargo...p. 14.
[42] Cuban Exiles... p. 5.

belonging to many foreign nationals including the U.S. citizens. Castro took oil refineries belonging to ESSO and Shell.[43]

Even law-abiding Cubans were not exempt from this madness. One such local farmer recounts that his productive and prosperous henequen fields (hemp, grown for rope fibers) were taken "for the good of the revolution." In return, he was issued worthless stock and empty promises of management.[44] This expropriation even captured hospitality industry giant Conrad Hilton's 25 story, 500 room Habana Hilton,[45] which the revolutionary regime set up his provisional headquarters for several months.

Among these expropriations were programs that cut the prices of the Cuban Electric Company (then majority-owned by the United States) and nationalized the U.S.-owned subsidiary of the International Telephone and Telegraph Corporation. But the most controversial measure was the Agrarian Reform Law of 1959 that prohibited latifundia, limited landholding to thirty cabellerías (approximately ninety-five acres) and expropriated all larger estates—redistributing them in

---

[43] Cuban Exiles… p. 6.
[44] Cuban Exiles… p. 20.
[45] Rosenberg, C. B. (2016). A "BIT" About Cuba - Using Bilateral Investment Treaties to Protect International Investments. Retrieved November 25, 2016, from http://www.hotelexecutive.com/about p. 1. Hilton invested $24 million in 1958 ($205 million in 2016). ("Rosenberg")

sections to private owners and small cooperatives. Castro ended large-scale private sector enterprise on the island, where the government assumed control of the banking industry; nearly 400 foreign and locally owned properties; and a total of 2.7 million acres of sugar lands. The law also stated that effective one year after its enactment, U.S.-owned sugar companies operating within Cuba had to be registered and owned by Cubans. In general, all businesses owned and operated by U.S. citizens or companies were nationalized, and taxes on imports from the United States were increased.[46]

As the property taking grew, an increasing number of Americans and Cubans fled the island. This began the growing brain drain as most Cuban professionals left for the U.S. and elsewhere.[47] The nationalism totaled over $1.9 billion.

1.5. *American Acts of Aggression Toward Cuba (Terrorism?)*

The United Nations General Assembly overwhelmingly and unequivocally condemned as criminal, all acts, methods and practices of terrorism wherever and whomever committed."[48] For years, the international community has tried unsuccessfully to define terrorism.

---

[46] Perez…p. 8.
[47] Cuban Exiles… p. 20.
[48] Paust, J. J., M., V. D., & Malone, L. A. (2005). International law and litigation in the U.S. St. Paul, MN: Thomson/West. ("Paust") p. 873.

In 1996, the General Assembly established an ad hoc committee to develop a comprehensive legal framework for dealing with international terrorism.[49] Accordingly the ad hoc committee, developed ways to suppress the financing of terrorism. Not until after the attacks on September 11, 2001, was a definition derived. Nearly by consensus, the working group defined,[50] "Terrorism is an act intended to cause death or serious bodily injury to any person; or serious damage to a State or government facility... when the purpose of such act, by its nature or context, is to intimidate a population, or to compel a Government or an international organization to do or abstain from doing an act. According to Professor Paust a working definition of terrorism has to include 1) an intent to produce terror and terror outcomes and 2) elimination purpose.[51]

Using these definitions, was the Bay of Pigs state sponsored terrorism or preventive self-defense like the USS Caroline? Was Operation Mongoose a litany of state sponsored terrorism against Cuba? Was Cuba rightfully seeking out the Soviet Union to defend herself by allowing the placement of Russian ballistic missiles on the island? When Castro encouraged Cuban Americans to flood America with immigration was this a terrorist

---

[49] Paust... p. 873.
[50] Paust... p. 875.
[51] Paust... p. 877.

act? Was the U.S. embargo over Cuba a terrorist act? Was the extraterritorial effect of Helms-Burton an act of economic terrorism? Was the Brothers to the Rescue dropping of leaflets urging revolts and insurgencies over Cuba and crossing into their airspace an act of terrorism?

1.5.1 BAY OF PIGS

The 1960s was a decade of particular conflict between the two countries as the United States pursued several attempts to overthrow the Cuban government. The first of these attempts was the Bay of Pigs Invasion in 1961, a military invasion of Cuba launched by the U.S. Central Intelligence Agency. The invasion, which was intended to be a secret, failed quite publicly less than twenty-four hours after it began.[52]

One of the Cuban American veterans of the disaster gives his recount. Alberto Martinez Echenique, a 75-year-old warrior and dissident from Bay of Pigs remembers Fidel Castro from the early years in High School, where Fidel was known as a "hothead."[53] Echenique passionately describes his love for Cuba as so much so that he packed up and joined the Brigade 2056[54] even though he had three small children at

---

[52] Perez... p. 8.
[53] Cuban Exiles... p. 30.
[54] Commonly referred to as Brigada 2056, which was a Brigade of Cuban exiles.

home.

He describes his return to Cuba as that of a patriot of his homeland ready to reclaim her for the Cuban people from the tyrannical grasp of Castro regime. He further explains that with the light, quick, maneuverable vehicles that the U.S. government supplied, the Brigade 2056's initial invasion was a rout because the *procastristas* were no match with their old, leftover slow WWII Stalin tanks and were sinking in the fine sand of the Cuban beaches.[55] As the battle raged on, he feels his brigade was moments from winning the battle and impeding victory but had outrun the lines of communication because President Kennedy had reneged on providing logistics, air-support, and reinforcement. He defined the heartbreaking frustration as, "Grown men standing around with what was an impressive amount of armaments for that era, but with no ammunition for it." Men were standing around crying and confused about the promised support that never arrived.[56]

1.5.2 Operation Mongoose

As a follow-up to the fiasco and humiliation of the "Bay of Pigs" in November 1961, President Kennedy

---
[55] Cuban Exiles… pp. 32-33.
[56] Cuban Exiles… p. 33.

authorized integrated covert operations against Cuba called Operation Mongoose.[57] The Cuban Project as it was also known had a two-prong approach 1) overthrow the Castro-led Communist regime and 2) establish a friendly government with which the U.S. could live in peace.[58] Pursuant to this project of synchronized terrorism, the CIA conducted covert attacks on electric power plants, an oil refinery, a sugar mill, and multiple assassination attempts on Castro. Later declassified documents revealed that the CIA provided funding to the Cuban Representation in Exile, who also attacked a Cuban ship in the Port of Vera Cruz in Mexico.[59]

1.5.3 Cuban Missile Crisis

One year later, in 1962, the revolutionary government sought assistance from the Soviet Union, and by the summer of that same year, the Soviets started placing missiles in Cuba. After tense negotiations between Moscow and Washington, D.C., Moscow offered to remove the missiles from Cuba if the United States promised not to invade Cuba again and remove nuclear armament from Turkey and Italy; the United States agreed. This thirteen-day confrontation between the United States and the Soviet Union is commonly

---

[57] Bacardi... p. 20.
[58] Bacardi... p. 20.
[59] Bacardi... p. 22.

referred to as the Cuban Missile Crisis.[60]

After Kennedy was assassinated, efforts in the 70s looked as if they were going to improve the relationship between the two nations. These efforts by U.S. President Jimmy Carter did not last long, however, and by 1980 the United States had returned to its former policies of diplomatic and economic isolation, containment, and clandestine activities.

1.5.4 Cuban Americans Influence on Foreign Policy

Like most of Latin American culture, Cubans, whether in Cuba or in America, subscribe to a phenomenon called *La Pena*,[61] whereby the open discussions are conducted in a civilized manner. This tradition has been largely unchanged throughout the years, continuing to provide a venue for discussions and sharing of thoughts, ideas, and even opposing views. Today, ground rules and decorum have been added to the format to maintain the open dialogue necessary to allow for civility in a room with competing ideas and opposing passionate thoughts.[62] It is in this setting that some argue that the U.S. foreign policy on Cuba is created.

---

[60] Perez... p. 8.
[61] Cuban Exiles... p 60. Translated to "large rock." The tradition dates as far back as 300 years to Spanish men of letters and poets and other learned individuals would gather at some readily identifiable locations such as a tree or perhaps a big rock.
[62] Cuban Exiles... p. 60.

La Pena can happen almost anywhere (coffee shops, produce markets, chess table), but one such place of significance for some Cuban Americans in South Florida is Miami-Dade Community College in the heart of Little Havana. The themes of this *pena*, almost always "revolve around Cuba, Cubans, and life both on the island and in exile." Imagine a diverse room of Cuban Americans with a smattering of *guayaberas*,[63] composed of a diverse age verbalizing their opinions with convictions engaging in intellectual duals with one another for a holistic approach to solving Cuba related issues.

Traditionally, the Cubans (whether exiled or on the island, once a Cuban always a Cuban) line up on either side of the argument: *procastrista* or *anticastrista*. The *anticastrista* group can be further broken down into *dialogeros*, who though they vehemently oppose the Castro regime, still firmly believe that a dialogue must be initiated and maintained with the Cuban people on the island including the Castro regime.[64]

In a Coral Gables pena, co-directed by one such *dialogeros* voice, Dr. Virgillo Beato, former head of school of medicine in Cuba,[65] galvanizes support for

---

[63] The traditional Cuban shirt.
[64] Cuban Exiles... p. 63.
[65] Cuban Exiles... p. 73. According to the author, Dr. Beato is remembered by the legions of Cuban doctors whom he trained before leaving the island.

moderation, where he has promoted dialogue and of establishing cohesion with the anticastrista factions. Dr. Beato reasons that in order to defeat communism, "we must all know and understand what communism is." Dr. Beato warns that [Fidel] "Castro [and presumably his brother, Raul] must not be dismissed as an idiot." Dr. Beato went on to caution that Castro "has been able to maintain an absolute control over Cuba for more than four decades."[66] Some argue this spirit of debate created the origins of the CANF.

1.5.5 Cuban-American National Foundation

According to most media reports and presumptions, President Reagan's first National Security Adviser and former CIA agent, Richard Allen[67] created CANF under the American Israel Public Affairs Committee (AIPAC) model.[68] The founding members were three Miami businessmen (Mas, Masvidal, and Salman) with Jose Mas Canosa as its original leader and longtime Executive Director.[69]

---

[66] Cuban Exiles… p. 75.
[67] The Miami Herald even referred to CANF as 'the brainchild of Richard Allen.'
[68] Though President Reagan is largely accredited with the downfall of the Soviet Union and communism, once the Iran-Contra story broke critics attacked the Reagan Doctrine to Latin America not only for the substance of the policies but the methods of instituting those policies. Arthur Schlesinger argued that Reagan doctrine's covert actions made secrecy, deceit, and mendacity the fundamental tenets of American foreign policy.
[69] Cuban Exiles… p. 34.

CANFs functioned through their main political activities. In the Reagan administration, CANF organized into separate branches for research, lobbying, and funding organizations. Next, CANF established Radio Marti or Radio Free Cuba. Authors Haney and Vanderbush argue that CANF also developed a special relationship with the National Endowment for Democracy (NED) to capture funding that was disbursed to Cuban human rights groups.[70] In 1991, CANF became eligible to receive $588 federal funds for each Cuban immigrant in an exodus support program designed to reunite more than 10,000 Cuban refugees. CANF also received $1.7 million from Department of Human Health and Services from a Cuban Exodus Relief Fund program. Lastly, CANF has extended its political savvy outside of Miami and even outside the U.S. For instance, when an exile outlines the CANF cause to a Congressman whose electorate apathetic in the Cuban question, then it isn't hard for CANF to convince this legislature by bolstering his campaign finances. Overall, the CANF seems to be a remarkably well-run organization its ability to lead, organize, fundraise, and lobby.

Some critics of CANF argue that the organization focuses on self-interest and its own power. For example, Dr. Elpidio Perez, a Cuban-born lawyer, believes that the

---

[70] Cuban Embargo... p. 44.

Cuban American National Foundation is a great organization for lobbying Congress but it unfortunately, more so protects its own interests here in the U.S. with only a cursory consideration of the Cuban problem Fidel Castro [and communism].[71]

1.5.6 *Immigration Crisis*

In summer 1994, a burgeoning group of desperate fleeing Cubans hi-jacked and commandeered tugboats, ferries, and even Navy passenger transport ships enroot to the U.S. With the occasional U.S. Coast Guard assistance, the hijackers would later be given political asylum in Miami.[72] In response, Cuba announced that henceforth Cubans were free to leave and thousands of balseros, or rafters, proceeded to leave on whatever rafts they could build, which caused a U.S. immigration crisis. To counter this, President Clinton ordered the Coast Guard to intercept them at sea and transport them to Guantanamo Naval Base. Thus, the "wet foot/dry foot" policy was born, whereby Cubans would still receive special status if they reached shore but not if intercepted at sea.

1.5.7 *The Initial Codification of the Embargo*

The U.S. policy against Cuba was strengthened with the Cuban Democracy Act in 1992, which prohibited travel

---

[71] Cuban Exiles… p. 54.
[72] Cuban Embargo… p. 95

to Cuba by U.S. citizens, family remittances to Cuba and foreign based subsidiaries of U.S. companies from trading with Cuba. Congressman Robert Torricelli's, the author of the legislation, apparent goal was to expedite the collapse of the Castro government through an economic noose tightening. The CDA's elimination of subsidiary trade was the most far reaching extra-territorial law regarding Cuba with fines of upwards of $1 million and up to ten years imprisonment.[73]

1.6. The Changing Tide of Americans of non-Cuban Descent

The 1990's were largely the same, but President Clinton did observe, "U.S. Foreign Policy with Cuba is controlled by a small percentage of Cuban Americans in Miami. Domestically, the Helms-Burton act wasn't garnering much support outside a certain segment of the Cuban-American population, the American public became increasingly vocal against the embargo. By 1995, even conservative pundits including John McLaughlin concluded that the embargo should be lifted or easing of sanctions or at least the initiation of serious dialogue with the Castro government. Religious groups dogged the administration for denying the shipment of a humanitarian bus to Cuba. Well, the tide was changing, until the HAR planes were shot down.

---

[73] Anatomy… p. 150.

1.7. Brothers to the Rescue

On February 24, 1996, Cuban Air Force MiG jetfighters shot down two unarmed Brothers to the Rescue (Hermanos al Rescate- "HAR") planes that had flown across the Florida straits toward Cuba, killing four Cuban Americans[74]. Many outraged by this act said that the HAR was simply flying overhead to provide humanitarian aid assistance to stranded rafters. While critics argue that there was a far from altruistic agenda taking shape, as HAR had been known to fly over Cuba and drop leaflets encouraging acts of civil disobedience and insurgency.[75]

Irrespective of Clinton's earlier observation of the irrational influence that South Floridians held over American foreign policy, the Helms-Burton Act became the apex of Cuba's policy. The CDA restrictions did not seem to be enough, however, and in 1996 Congress enacted the Cuban Liberty and Democratic Solidarity Act,[76] which essentially extended the territorial application of the Cuba Democracy Act. Foreign companies were prohibited from trading with Cuba, and foreign companies trading in property previously owned by U.S. citizens, but confiscated by Cuba after the Cuban

---

[74] Cuban Embargo… p. 99.
[75] Bacardi… p. 61.
[76] Also, commonly referred to as the Helms-Burton Act.

Revolution, would be penalized.[77]

1.8. Extraterritorial Application

This law punished foreign companies that do business with Cuba and reserves the president international foreign policy prerogative.[78] Title III of Helms-Burton provides a cause of action in a U.S. court against anyone who traffics sells, transfers, distributes, manages, or otherwise disposes of, purchases, leases, etc…. property expropriated by the Cuban government on or after January 1, 1959. In essence, the U.S. is exercising extra-territorial jurisdiction over actions of a foreign company that took place on foreign soil, for someone who was not a U.S. citizen at the time of the loss.[79]

The International Community was swift to criticize the reach of the Helms-Burton act. The European Union stated that it cannot accept the United States creating unilateral legislation to determine and restrict the EU's economic and commercial relations. Canada and Mexico were in staunch opposition to the act and issued blocking orders to prevent their companies from obeying U.S. extraterritorial laws.[80] The EU brought an action against the Helms-Burton legislation before the World Trade Organization arguing that the law was

---

[77] Perez…p. 8.
[78] Anatomy… p. 180.
[79] Anatomy… p. 180.
[80] Anatomy… p. 184.

illegal under international trade rules. Mexico and Canada initiated a complaint against the U.S. under NAFTA.[81] The Organization of American States unanimously found that the Helms-Burton was repugnant to international law. The Pope called the legislation "oppressive economic measures, unjust and ethically unacceptable, imposed from outside the country." The UN voted against the legislation 143 to 3, in favor of Cuba.[82]

The international community, the hemispheric community, Cuban exiles, Cubans, and Americans asked four main embargo related questions: 1) How effective is the trade Embargo; 2) How the Embargo affects the common Cuban;[83] 3) Does its extraterritorial nature and application injure friendly nations; and 4) When will it the sanctions end?

Pursuant to the sanctions theory analysis, the embargo or blockade of Cuba has no more usefulness and should be discontinued. First, as the sanction theory heeds sanctions tend to be a unifying force in the targeted country meaning non-fleeing Cubans are likely to rally around the Castro government. Another warning under the sanctions theory is that collateral economic harm caused to third parties render the sanctions

---

[81] Anatomy... p. 185.
[82] Anatomy... p. 186.
[83] Cuban Exiles... p. 1.

unsuccessful. The Helms-Burton evoked unprecedented condemnation. Third, a lack of support on the home front by influential constituencies diminishes the sanctions chance of success. Finally, the strengthening of hard-liners in the sanctions target government can be an unintended consequence. As the case in Cuba, before the Helms-Burton, potential Cuban reformers voice was squelched when both the American people and International community sided with Cuba.

1.8.1 Why a BIT can help a bit? From Gunboat Diplomacy to Bilateral Investment Treaties

Ever since Adam Smith there has been virtual unanimity among economists, whatever their ideological position on other issues, that international free trade is in the best interests of trading countries and of the world.[84] As the United States became a military power in the first decade of the 20th century, the "Rooseveltian" version of gunboat diplomacy, Big Stick Diplomacy, was superseded by dollar diplomacy: replacing the big stick with the "juicy carrot" of American private investment or bilateral investment treaties to reduce chances of aggression with other nation states.

1.8.2 BITs Historically

---

[84] Milton Friedman

The concept of negotiating treaties aimed specifically at the promotion and protection of foreign investment originated in Germany. The first BIT was signed between the Federal Republic of Germany and Pakistan on November 25, 1959.[85]

The use of BITs developed slowly at first. Over the period 1959-69, only 75 BITs were concluded worldwide, while 92 were concluded in the 1970s. In the 1980s, however, the debt crisis forced countries that had relied on foreign loans for development financing to turn to foreign direct investment (FDI) as an important source of capital. As a result, developing countries began to encourage foreign investors to locate within their borders and signed BITs as a way to signify their willingness to accept foreign participation in their economies.[86]

The '80s saw 219 BITs signed, including a significant number between developing countries as well as the first BITs signed by China and by the United States. An additional 946 BITs were signed between 1990 and 1996. At the end of 1996, developed countries had signed 924 BITs (62 percent of the total number of BITs), while developing countries and economies in transition

---

[85] Perez-Lopez, J. F., & Travieso-Díaz, M. F. (2016). The Contribution of BITs to Cuba's Foreign Investment Program. Retrieved November 25, 2016, from http://www.ascecuba.org/ ("Perez-Lopez") p. 456.
[86] Pérez-López... p. 457.

had signed 508 (38 percent).

The boom in BITs in the 1990s is attributable to a several factors.[87] This non-exhaustive list includes the opening to foreign investment brought about by changes toward a global market economy in the former socialist countries of Eastern and Central Europe and in the newly independent states of the former Soviet Union. Additionally, the recognition among developing countries of the positive role in economic development that can be played by FDI and the intense competition among countries to attract FDI. Freedom of self-determination comes at the cost of self-sufficiency, the issue then becomes how to fund self-rule. With the burgeoning of all of the newly independent nations, shrinkages in foreign aid generally, and difficulties on the part of many developing countries in obtaining additional foreign financing via debt fostered a BIT friendly environment.[88] The consensus among developed and developing countries, as well as transition economies, that it is in a country's national interest to provide increased legal protection to FDI.

1.8.3 BITs Protection from an International Perspective

To understand Bilateral Investment Protection in global commercial activities, one must first determine the

---

[87] Pérez-López... p. 458.
[88] Pérez-López... p. 458.

overarching world governing authority as it relates to trade. Since there is no "Code of International Law," governments and businesses alike should look to the sources of international law.[89] According to Professor Christopher Greenwood, "While there is an International Court of Justice and a range of specialized international courts and tribunals, their jurisdiction is critically dependent upon the consent of States and they lack what can properly be described as a compulsory jurisdiction of the kind possessed by national courts." The non-exhaustive list of sources of law for the 192 internationally nation-states[90] include the following:

(a) Treaties between States;
(b) Customary international law derived from the practice of States;
(c) General principles of law recognized by civilized nations; and, as subsidiary means for the determination of rules of international law:
(d) Judicial decisions and the writings of "the most highly qualified publicists".

After Chavez' expropriation of the energy industry in Venezuela, foreign investors scrambled for ways to protect their investments. Pursuant to the concept of *lex*

---

[89] Sources of International Law: An Introduction by Professor Christopher Greenwood
[90] The Statute of the International Court of Justice, Art. 38

mercatoria,[91] the ICSID proceeding between Exxon/Mobil Corporation vs. Venezuela, the tribunal held that Mobil's aim at restructuring their investments in Venezuela through a Dutch holding was to protect their rights by the Venezuelan authorities by gaining access to ICSID arbitration through a BIT. The tribunal opined that this was a perfectly legitimate goal as far as it concerned future disputes.[92] Moreover, the rules of international law governing the expropriation of alien property have long been of central concern to foreigners in general and to foreign investors in particular. Expropriation is the most severe form of interference with property, and if the investment is taken without adequate compensation, all expectations of the

---

[91] "[I]n international relations, the tribunal considers that it is preferable to apply rules adapted to the conditions of the international market and which provide a reasonable balance between the company's confidence in its distinct legal status and the protection of entities which may fall victim to the manipulations of a company controlling its subsidiary to deprive a creditor of the benefits to which it is entitled... The application of international principles offers many advantages. They apply in a uniform fashion and are independent from the peculiarities of each national law. They take into consideration the needs of international relations and allow for a fruitful exchange between systems which are sometimes excessively attached to conceptual distinctions, and systems which seek a just and pragmatic solution to particular situations. This is therefore an ideal opportunity to apply what is increasingly referred to as the *lex mercatoria*." Rules Adapted To the Conditions of the International Market / Lex Mercatoria. Award in Case14208/14236 page 4.

[92] ICSID CASE No. ARB 07/27- The Tribunal opined that it had jurisdiction under the ICSID Convention and the BIT with respect to any dispute born after 21 February 2006 for the Cerro Negro project and after 23 November 2006 for the La Ceiba project, and in particular with respect to the pending dispute relating to the nationalization of the investments.

investors are destroyed.[93]

Notwithstanding the exceptional nature of taking foreign property, a nation state is still a sovereign and has certain rights in the international community. According to two of the world's most renowned international law scholars, Rudolf Dolzer and Christoph Schreuer, the host state's right to expropriate alien property in principle is consistent with the notion of territorial sovereignty and accepted pursuant to the classical rules of international law. Dolzer and Schreuer describe the three branches that international law has developed that regulate the scope and conditions of the exercise of this power. The first one defines the interests or investments that will be protected.[94] Additionally, the second branch requires defining expropriation, which can provide a high degree of complexity when the host state interferes with title rights of the foreign owner without a formal taking of title, i.e., "creeping expropriation." The third branch of expropriation law relates to the conditions under which a state expropriates alien property in whether or not the foreign entity was justly compensated. Most recently states have been reluctant to conduct wholesale expropriation due to the sweeping and chilling effect

---

[93] Dolzer, Rudolf, and Christoph Schreuer. Principles of International Investment Law. Oxford: Oxford UP, 2008. ("Dolzer")
[94] Dolzer... p. 99.

that it has on its future foreign investments.[95] These notions must be considered in a proposed BIT between Cuba and the U.S.

As an independent way of investigating appropriateness and non-discriminatory grounds for state confiscation, then look to investor-state tribunals, like ICSID and others. Investor-state tribunals have wide jurisdiction to interpret and apply the substantive provisions of investment treaties. State-to-state tribunals have limited jurisdiction over residual issues, such as the failure of a state to pay an investor-state award. In light of their growing dissatisfaction with the investment treaty system, many states have sought to reengage with the field in multiple ways in an effort to influence its development.

As part of this process, a number of state-to-state arbitrations have been launched, including: (1) diplomatic protection claims made by home states seeking compensation on behalf of their investors; (2) interpretive disputes about the proper interpretation of investment treaties; and (3) requests for declaratory relief seeking a finding that the treaty has or has not

---

[95] Dolzer... p. 98.

been violated.[96]

Consider the facts of Argentina in 2001 in their dire economic conditions when the officials resorted to enacting wide-ranging regulatory reforms, resulting in more than forty investor-state arbitrations being filed on an already over taxed government. Should all of the countries that Argentina have BITs with engage in state-state arbitration to diplomatically assist a fellow nation-state get back on its feet? Would this state-to-state arbitration be viewed as a dangerous development that threatens to infringe upon investors' rights and to re-politicize investor-state disputes?[97] Do these investors have a reasonable expectation of support from their own Ministry of Foreign Affairs or State Department?

Speaking of expectations, let's look at legitimate expectations in terms of fair and equitable treatment ("FET") in government takings. In *Tecmed v. Mexico*,[98] which is said to be "the award most often cited in arbitral jurisprudence." Its popularity likely lies in its

---

[96] Roberts, A., (2014) State-to-State Investment Treaty Arbitration: A Hybrid Theory of Interdependent Rights and Shared Interpretive Authority. Harvard International Law Journal, 55(1), 1. ("Roberts") p. 3.
[97] Roberts... p. 4.
[98] Reed, Lucy, and Simon Consedine. "Chapter 20: Fair and Equitable Treatment: Legitimate Expectations and Transparency." Kluwer Arbitration Blog. N.p., 2000. Web. 30 Nov. 2016. The Tribunal awarded Tecmed USD 5.5 million in damages plus 6% annual interest from November 1998. Tecmed had sought USD 52 million, based on a discounted cash flow analysis to assess the market value of the landfill at the time of the expropriation.

offering of a conceptual framework for evaluating the otherwise amorphous FET protection. According to Tecmed, tribunals should evaluate whether the host government acted (i) consistently, (ii) with a lack of ambiguity, and (iii) transparently in its dealings with the investor. Moreover, this evaluation should be applied both to the host State's actions and the goals that motivate them.[99]

1.9. Cuba's Foreign Investment Protections

1.9.1 Cuba's Expropriation Model:

Few countries match the expropriatory model of revolutionary Cuba. The nearly 6,000 claims filed in the United States were valued by the Foreign Claims Settlement Commission as of 1972 at US$1.8 billion. Described by one scholar as the "largest uncompensated taking of American property by a foreign government in history," the expropriations touched virtually every industry on the island. [100] This yielded lasting skepticism of foreign investments in the island.

Under the Fidel Castro's brand of anti-capitalism, he vehemently opposed globalization. Anti-globalization is diametrically opposed to international investments

---

[99] *Tecmed v. Mexico*, ICSID Case No. ARB(AF)/00/2
[100] Infante, E. R., & Samra, H. J. (2016) Back to the Future? Foreign Investment Protection in Cuba. International Law Quarterly, 32(3), 18. ("Infante")

because foreign investors must be sure that they have certain tools in place to protect their carefully planned investment. These protections have bolstered the expansion of foreign direct investment (FDI) in developing countries from $14B in 1985 to $681B in 2014. On February 19, 2008, Granma published Fidel Castro's message announcing due to his poor health, he could no longer serve as President of Cuba. Therefore, when the National Assembly of People's Power (Cuba's legislative body) convened to elect Raul Castro, a pragmatist, word traveled fast that this may allow for change for allowing potential foreign investors.[101] This bodes well for Cuba in that the current mindset of international scholars is that there is a new transnational order whereby arbitral tribunals and their network of decisions are dictating the terms to sovereigns.[102]

Fast forward to 2014, Cuba enacted the Foreign Investment Act (FIA), which updated the legal framework governing investments to offer greater

---

[101] Guerra, G. (2008). Cuba: Legal Implications of the Resignation of the Cuban President. Retrieved November 25, 2016, from http://www.loc.gov/law/
[102] "THE NEW WORLD ORDER OF ECONOMIC RELATIONS IN THE LIGHT OF ARBITRAL JURISPRUDENCE" Submitted by Alfredo De Jesús O., and José Ricardo Feris at the Beaune Meeting of September 27, 2014. The new world order of economic relations emerges as a consequence of the impact of globalization along with the progressive decline of the theoretical models that placed the Nation-State at the center of the economy and the rule of law. This new world order may be ascertained by the observation of three phenomenon: the globalization of the economy, the globalization of contract law and the globalization of arbitration law.

incentives to foreign investors and provide substantive protections to foreign investments. The FIA recognizes three distinct forms of foreign investments: (i) joint venture companies with Cuban partners; (ii) international economic association contracts, which include management and professional services contracts; and (iii) 100% foreign owned companies.

For example, in the tourism sector, Cuba has generally required new hotels to provide some ownership or management rights to the Cuban government.[103] In addition, Cuba has concluded 40 bilateral investment treaties (BITs), which are international treaties between two countries that protect international investments. The full list of these countries is shown below. These 40 countries include 12 members of the G20 and twelve members of the EU.

As a developing country, Cuba reportedly has a GDP of $81B,[104] and has laid out its 2014 "Portfolio Opportunities for Foreign Investment,"[105] which lists over $8B in 246 specified development projects. Cuban Law 118, the foreign investment law offers favorable conditions in principle but implementing the regulations

---

[103] Rosenberg… p. 2.
[104] In terms of size, there is current proposed acquisition/ merger of Time Warner by AT&T for approximately $86B.
[105] Feinberg… p. 68.

seems to be a bit elusive for some.[106] To understand the mixed signals of the black letter regulation and the Castro government implementation is easily understood if one looks at the Law 118 and the attitudes of Cubans toward foreign investors.[107] This chart below illustrates Cuba's attitude toward the foreign investment model.

PHASE 1	PHASE 2	PHASE 3	PHASE 4	PHASE 5
Revolutionary	Post-Soviet	Conservative	Socialist	Ambivalent
1960s	1990s	2000s	Mid-to-late 2000s	2011-present
Nationalism and Expropriation	Liberalization and welcome	Retrenchment And cancellations	SOE partners (Venezuela, China, Brazil)	Economic reform; anticorruption campaign

Figure 4-1. Five Phases of Cuban policies toward Foreign Direct Investment.[108]

The Cuban government's skepticism may be rationale considering their economic dependency failures. First, they depended on Spain, who ruled with an iron fist. Then after the Spanish American War victory, Cuba became a U.S. protectorate, a de facto U.S. colony, with

---
[106] Feinberg... p. 71.
[107] Cristina Escobar Domínguez advised that Cubans attitudes towards foreign investors were cautiously optimistic.
[108] Feinberg... p. 71.

no ability to treaty or borrow, so when the "Great Depression" struck the U.S., it drowned Cuba. Then again, during the Cold War, Cuba bet on the Soviet Union, when that debacle crashed, the island nation fell into a "Special Period." When Venezuela decreased international subsidies due to drastically falling oil prices, Cubans looked to China. In the China partnership, Cuba found a trade imbalance of about $1B. Therefore, maybe the Castro regime is warranted in their skepticism of letting American businesses enter too rapidly and without control.

1.9.2 Cuba's take on Foreign Investments and BITs

Cuba had prohibited foreign investment in the island in the 1960s, and it was not until 1982 that Cuba enacted new legislation allowing foreign investment through joint ventures between Cuban enterprises and foreign entities. This new legislation did not generate the foreign investment the island needed. So, in September 1995, Cuba adopted Law No. 77 on Foreign Investment allowing the signing of more than forty foreign investment treaties from 1995 to 1999, which in turn resulted in significant foreign investment in Cuba.[109]

From the Cuban government's point of view, the critical challenge facing General Castro is to balance the need to

---

[109] Perez... p. 8.

improve the economy and satisfy the needs of the population while maintaining continuous political control because rapid economic reforms may lead to a loosening of political control.[110]

1.9.3 The BIT from the Cuban Perspective

Before committing resources, U.S. investors are increasingly exploring the current legal regime[111] and questioning whether their investments will be safe. As explained below, Cuba's investment protection framework is surprisingly robust, though there are serious questions about the de facto protections actually afforded to U.S. and other investors. There is an astronomical difference between writing legislation and implementing true protection.[112] Cuban government has entered into sixty bilateral investment treaties with countries around the world. Of these treaties, more than two-thirds are in force. Cuba also features a newly implemented foreign investment law. Despite these reforms, incremental change remains the most likely scenario.[113]

---

[110] Suchlicki, Jaime. (2016) Challenges for Investors in Cuba. International Law Quarterly, 32(3), 14. ("Suchlicki")
[111] Cuba's regulatory framework for foreign investment consists of (1) the above-mentioned Law No. 77; (2) decrees and regulations implementing that law; and (3) some complementary legislation, such as the tax code, a new mining law, and reforms to the banking system.
[112] Infante... p. 18.
[113] Infante... p. 18.

In Cuba, BITs serve to complement this limited legal framework. For instance, Foreign Investment Law No. 77 codified the rules under which enterprises that included foreign participation had been operating and introduced some innovations to the legal framework for foreign investment. Among them for example, wholly-owned foreign investments, unlike the previous legislation,[114] Law No. 77 allows for the possibility of investments that are 100 percent-owned by foreigners.

According to Cristina Escobar Dominguez' perspective,[115] this is a simplified approval process: Law No. 77 streamlines the administrative approval process for foreign investments.[116] For example, for relatively small and non-sensitive investments, case-by-case approval by the Executive Committee of the Council of Ministers is no longer required, with the approval decision relegated to a Government Commission appointed by the Executive Council. Similarly, pursuant to Law No. 77, a decision on whether to approve a foreign investment must be handed down within 60 days from the date on which the request was presented; no time frame for

---

[114] Previous Cuban legislation, limited foreign investors to 49 percent ownership in joint ventures with domestic (state) investors.

[115] National Cuban Journalist and Reporter, Cuban Institute of Radio and Television, Cuba, who is most prominently featured as a Cuban rising star............ in her talk at the Baker Institute and an outspoken supporter of the Cuban government.

[116] Ms. Dominguez opined that these are significant changes and U.S. businesses should be patient be willing to enter through the process.

handing down such decision was specified in the previous legislation.

All sectors[117] of the economy are open to foreign investment, subject to approval procedures, with the exception of health and education services and national defense (other than commercial enterprises of the armed forces).

1.9.4 Domestic Protection Offered to the Foreign Investors

In the months preceding President Obama's announced policy changes, the Cuban government implemented its own significant reforms directed at promoting foreign investment and adopted the new Ley No. 118 *de Inversión Extranjera*. The Ley de Inversión's liberalization of foreign investment has been recognized by numerous commentators. Most notably, the reform explicitly

---

[117] **Investments in real estate:**
Law No. 77 for the first time permits foreign investments in the real estate sector. However, such foreign investments are limited to:
(1) housing or tourism facilities for the use of persons who are not permanent residents of Cuba;
(2) purchase of real estate for corporate activities; and
(3) real estate development for the tourism industry.
Incentives for investments in export processing zones:
Law No. 77 foresees the designation, by the Executive Committee of the Council of Ministers, of areas in the national territory where duty-free zones or industrial parks might operate. The law further provides that certain incentives may be offered to investors who locate in these areas.
Ability to export and import:
Joint ventures or wholly foreign-owned enterprises are given the right, in accordance with domestic legislation "to export their products directly and to import, also directly, whatever is needed to meet their needs."

authorizes foreign investment in all sectors—subject to government approval—except education, health care, and the military. Among the numerous changes implemented, the Ley de Inversión also cuts taxes imposed on foreign investment, explicitly permits wholly owned foreign investments, recognizes intellectual property rights and streamlines registration requirements. Promisingly, the Ley de Inversión incorporates several fundamental investment protection standards, including "full protection and security."

What does this mean exactly? Will Cuba subject itself to an international arbitration to settle a dispute? The most common form of dispute resolution and investor protection between states and foreign investors, international arbitration, was explicitly avoided. Rather, the law only provides a process for determining the appropriate level of compensation due when a direct expropriation occurs, an increasingly rare phenomenon. This power is vested in the appropriate Cuban Provincial Court with jurisdiction over the dispute.[118] American investors should tread very carefully in this environment.

Cuba's BIT network is geographically widespread and crosses an incredible number of boundaries, economies, governments, languages, and cultures. Cuba's

---

[118] Infante... p. 18.

investment treaties possess many of the key investment protections common to bilateral investment treaties around the world. These include full protection and security, fair and equitable treatment, national treatment, most-favored nation treatment, umbrella clauses and protections against expropriation. The UK-Cuba BIT, among the most expansive of Cuba's bilateral investment treaties, includes all of these protections. Although absent from the Ley de Inversión's law, many of Cuba's bilateral investment treaties include recourse to international arbitration.[119] Even though the BITs lack uniformity, Cuba does allow International Chamber of Commerce International Court of Arbitration ("ICC") arbitration and ad hoc arbitration under the United Nations Commission on International Trade Law ("UNCITRAL") rules for some BITs.

For example, the UK-Cuba BIT permits investors, after an initial notification and conciliation period, to submit claims to either the ICC or to ad hoc arbitration under the UNCITRAL rules. On the other hand, the Lebanon-Cuba BIT permits recourse either to the domestic courts or to ad hoc arbitration under the UNCITRAL rules. Cuba's bilateral investment treaties with Spain, Vietnam, Romania, Argentina, Greece, Slovakia, Barbados, Germany, Chile, the Netherlands and Venezuela follow

---

[119] Infante... p. 64.

the same pattern.[120] Broadly speaking, Cuba's efforts related to investment treaties and willingness to accede to international dispute resolution are confidence-building.

1.9.5 Cuban BIT Litigation

What happens in Cuba if or when Cuba can't pay or enacts "creeping" legislation that is tantamount to taking of foreign investments? Should the state get involved to protect the citizen's investments? Will ICSID or some other international tribunal hear the matter?

As an example, in *Italy v. Cuba*, Italy brought a claim on behalf of itself and several Italian investors alleging violations of the Cuba-Italy BIT. Italy contended that it had "double standing" to bring a direct claim (to vindicate its own substantive rights) and a diplomatic protection claim (to vindicate the rights of Italian nationals that had invested in Cuba. Cuba argued that the existence of an investor-state arbitration clause in the treaty prevented Italy from bringing a diplomatic protection claim. The tribunal rejected Cuba's argument but ultimately held that Italy's direct claim failed because its claim on behalf of its nationals failed.[121]

---

[120] Infante... p. 64.
[121] Roberts... p. 7. Citing *Republic of It. v. Republic of Cuba*, Sentence pr´eliminaire, [Interim Award] (Ad Hoc Arb. Trib. Mar. 15, 2005), available at http://italaw.com/sites/default/files/case-documents/ita0434_0.pdf [hereinafter

Ultimately, Cuba has entered a wide array of treaties to counter their last 56 years of over dependence on singular or limited economic partnerships. According to the United Nations Conference on Trade and Development (UNCTD), Cuba has 60 BITs and 3 Treaties with Investment Provisions.

Italy v. Cuba, Interim Award]; Republic of It. v. Republic of Cuba, Sentence finale [Final Award] (AdHoc Arb. Trib. Jan. 15, 2008), available at http://italaw.com/sites/default/files/case-documents/ita0435_0.pdf [hereinafter Italy v. Cuba, Final Award]

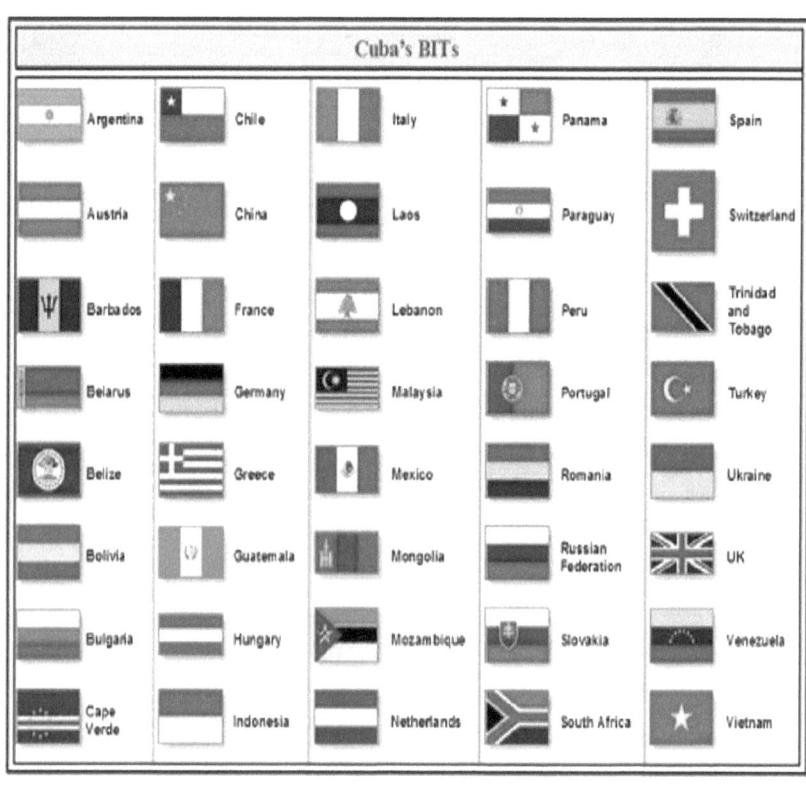

Figure 1 Flags Depicting Cuba BIT Trade Partners

CUBA
BILATERAL INVESTMENT TREATIES

No.	Title (Short Version)	Status	Date of signature	Date of entry into force
1	Algeria - Cuba BIT (1999)	In negotiation		
2	Argentina - Cuba BIT (1995)	In force	30/11/1995	01/06/1997
3	Austria - Cuba BIT (2000)	In force	19/05/2000	25/11/2001
4	Barbados - Cuba BIT (1996)	In force	19/02/1996	13/08/1998
5	Belarus - Cuba BIT (2000)	In force	08/06/2000	16/08/2001
6	Belize - Cuba BIT (1998)	In force	08/04/1998	16/04/1999
7	BLEU (Belgium-Luxembourg Economic	Signed	19/05/1998	
8	Bolivia, Plurinational State of - Cuba BIT	In force	06/05/1995	23/08/1998
9	Brazil - Cuba BIT (1997)	Signed	26/06/1997	
10	Bulgaria - Cuba BIT (1998)	In force	16/12/1998	24/05/2000
11	Cape Verde - Cuba BIT (1997)	In force	22/05/1997	08/01/2003
12	Cambodia - Cuba BIT (2001)	Signed	26/09/2001	
13	Chile - Cuba BIT (1996)	In force	10/01/1996	30/09/2000
14	China - Cuba BIT (1995)	In force	24/04/1995	01/08/1996
15	Colombia - Cuba BIT (1994)	Signed	16/07/1994	
16	Croatia - Cuba BIT (2001)	Signed	16/02/2001	
17	Cuba - Denmark BIT (2001)	Signed	19/02/2001	
18	Cuba - Dominican Republic BIT (1999)	Signed	15/11/1999	
19	Cuba - Ecuador BIT (1997)	Terminated	06/05/1997	15/08/1997
20	Cuba - Finland BIT (2001)	Signed	17/12/2001	
21	Cuba - France BIT (1997)	In force	25/04/1997	06/11/1999
22	Cuba - Germany BIT (1996)	In force	30/04/1996	22/11/1998
23	Cuba - Ghana BIT (1999)	Signed	02/11/1999	
24	Cuba - Greece BIT (1996)	In force	18/06/1996	18/10/1997
25	Cuba - Guatemala BIT (1999)	In force	20/08/1999	10/08/2002
26	Cuba - Guyana BIT (1999)	Signed	22/10/1999	
27	Cuba - Honduras BIT (2001)	Signed	09/08/2001	
28	Cuba - Hungary BIT (1999)	In force	22/10/1999	24/11/2003
29	Cuba - Indonesia BIT (1997)	In force	19/09/1997	29/09/1999
30	Cuba - Italy BIT (1993)	In force	07/05/1993	23/08/1995

CUBA
BILATERAL INVESTMENT TREATIES

31	Cuba - Jamaica BIT (1997)	Signed	31/05/1997	
32	Cuba - Lao People's Democratic Republic	In force	28/04/1997	10/06/1998
33	Cuba - Lebanon BIT (1995)	In force	14/12/1995	07/01/1999
34	Cuba - Malaysia BIT (1997)	In force	26/09/1997	27/10/1999
35	Cuba - Mexico BIT (2001)	In force	30/05/2001	29/03/2002
36	Cuba - Mongolia BIT (1999)	In force	26/03/1999	18/10/2000
37	Cuba - Mozambique BIT (2001)	In force	20/10/2001	26/02/2002
38	Cuba - Namibia BIT (1997)	Signed	27/06/1997	
39	Cuba - Netherlands BIT (1999)	In force	02/11/1999	01/11/2001
40	Cuba - Panama BIT (1999)	In force	27/01/1999	11/05/1999
41	Cuba - Paraguay BIT (2000)	In force	21/11/2000	06/12/2002
42	Cuba - Peru BIT (2000)	In force	10/10/2000	25/11/2001
43	Cuba - Portugal BIT (1998)	In force	08/07/1998	18/06/1999
44	Cuba - Qatar BIT (2001)	Signed	06/11/2001	
45	Cuba - Romania BIT (1996)	In force	27/01/1996	22/05/1997
46	Cuba - Russian Federation BIT (1993)	In force	07/07/1993	08/07/1996
47	Cuba - San Marino BIT (2002)	Signed	01/01/2002	
48	Cuba - Slovakia BIT (1997)	In force	22/03/1997	05/12/1997
49	Cuba - South Africa BIT (1995)	In force	08/12/1995	07/04/1997
50	Cuba - Spain BIT (1994)	In force	27/05/1994	09/06/1995
51	Cuba - Suriname BIT (1999)	Signed	07/01/1999	
52	Cuba - Switzerland BIT (1996)	In force	28/06/1996	07/11/1997
53	Cuba - Trinidad and Tobago BIT (1999)	In force	26/05/1999	07/01/2000
54	Cuba - Turkey BIT (1997)	In force	22/12/1997	23/10/1999
55	Cuba - Uganda BIT (2002)	Signed	01/01/2002	
56	Cuba - Ukraine BIT (1995)	In force	20/05/1995	04/12/1996
57	Cuba - United Kingdom BIT (1995)	In force	30/01/1995	11/05/1995
58	Cuba - Venezuela, Bolivarian Republic of	In force	11/12/1996	15/04/2004
59	Cuba - Viet Nam BIT (1995)	In force	12/10/1995	01/10/1996
60	Cuba - Zambia BIT (2000)	Signed	22/01/2000	

1.10. U.S.- Cuban Relations 2014 and Beyond[122]

Now that President Obama has visited so what, now what? What is the U.S. willing to do to enhance the relationship? How does Texas specifically Houston fit into this puzzle? The Department of the Treasury's Office of Foreign Assets Control (OFAC)[123] and the Department of Commerce's Bureau of Industry and Security (BIS) announced new amendments to the Cuban Assets Control Regulations (CACR) and Export Administration Regulations (EAR), respectively.

These amendments help create more economic opportunity for Cubans and Americans, further implementing the direction toward Cuba that President Obama laid out in December 2014. The changes took effect on October 17, 2016, when the regulations were published in the Federal Register. "President Obama's

---

[122] On Thursday, October 27, 2016, the Rice University Baker Institute for Public Policy hosted U.S.-Cuba Relations Beyond 2016: Trade, Investment and Political Outlooks. The event was co-sponsored by the Baker Institute Latin America Initiative and the International Law Section of the State Bar of Texas. The video can be viewed at www.bakerinstitute.org

[123] U.S. Department of the Treasury Frequently Asked Questions Related to Cuba. (2016, October 14). Retrieved November 25, 2016, from https://www.treasury.gov/ U.S DEPARTMENTS OF TREASURY AND COMMERCE ANNOUNCE FURTHER AMENDMENTS TO CUBA SANCTIONS REGULATIONS: Amendments Expand Venues for Scientific Collaboration, Facilitate Increased Humanitarian Support, and Bolster Trade and Commercial Opportunities

historic announcement in December 2014 charted a new course for a stronger, more open U.S.-Cuba relationship," said Treasury Secretary Jacob J. Lew. "The Treasury Department has worked to break down economic barriers in areas such as travel, trade and commerce, banking, and telecommunications." These actions build on this progress by enabling more scientific collaboration, grants and scholarships, people-to-people contact, and private sector growth. These steps have the potential to accelerate constructive change and unlock greater economic opportunity for Cubans and Americans.[124]

These changes are intended to expand opportunities for scientific collaboration by authorizing certain transactions related to Cuban-origin pharmaceuticals and joint medical research; improve living conditions for Cubans by expanding existing authorizations for grants and humanitarian related services; increase people-to-people contact in Cuba by facilitating authorized travel and commerce; facilitate safe travel between the United States and Cuba by authorizing civil aviation safety-related services; and bolster trade and commercial opportunities by expanding and streamlining

---

[124] These amendments will create more opportunities for Cuban citizens to access American goods and services, further strengthening the ties between our two countries," said U.S. Secretary of Commerce Penny Pritzker. "More commercial activity between the U.S. and Cuba benefits our people and our economies.

authorizations relating to trade and commerce. These amendments also implement certain technical and conforming changes. OFAC and BIS are making these amendments in support of the process of normalizing bilateral relations with Cuba.

1.10.1 So What for Texas?

This renewed relationship has particular importance to Texas,[125] which is a strong economic driver for the U.S. economy and could greatly benefit from open trade with Cuba. Last December, Texas Gov. Greg Abbott visited Cuba, and the Houston mayor's office and the Greater Houston Partnership went on a trade mission to the island in September 2016.

The Rice University's Baker Institute held a conference addressing the rapidly developing political, business and legal ties between the two countries. Experts from Cuba and the U.S. discussed political and economic outlooks, as well as the current investment framework in Cuba and the reforms necessary to facilitate trade and investment in the continuing environment of normalization.

---

[125] DESCRIPTION of the Conference: The relationship between Cuba and the United States is undergoing a historic transformation. In the months since Presidents Barack Obama and Raúl Castro announced that their countries would restore diplomatic relations, numerous measures have strengthened the bilateral relationship, including the reopening of embassies, the reestablishment of commercial flights, an ease in restrictions of certain imports and exports, and the facilitation of selected financial transactions.

After the Houston Mayor's office gave the scene setter and welcomed the attendees. The speakers and panelist engaged in productive dialogue on the way forward for both businesses and policy engagement with Cuba. With an introduction by Attorney Sashe D. Dimitroff,[126] a Partner at Baker Hostetler, the first speaker from Amherst College, Dr. Javier Corrales, discussed the "Old and New U.S.-Cuba Relationship." This oriented the less-familiar attendees to the tumultuous and sometimes very close ties that the two nations have shared. He offered insight into the domestic and hemispheric challenges to ongoing fruitless policy of 'non-engagement.' He additionally issued warnings of cautious optimism suggesting that businesses should evaluate the history and culture of each nation before recklessly dashing for this new opportunity.

In the second panel moderated by Dr. Pablo M. Pinto,[127] Professor Juan A. Triana[128] and Professor Jorge R. Piñón[129] opined on a "New Economic Relationship?" between the two nations. Professor Triana discussed the differences in societal expectations and economic

---

[126] Dimitroff is an adjunct professor at University of Houston Law Center and teaches International Risk Management, which focuses on the legal framework for international oilfield services contracts and international agreements, including both substantive law and practical counseling.

[127] Associate Professor of Political Science, University of Houston, and Nonresident Scholar, Baker Institute Latin America Initiative

[128] Professor, University of Havana, Cuba

[129] A Cuban American and the Director, Latin America and Caribbean Energy Program, The University of Texas at Austin.

realities. While Professor Pinon briefed the audience on regional economic opportunities between U.S., Cuba, and Mexico for the "Doughnut Hole" in the gulf waters, which is an oil-rich Eastern Polygon[130] in the Gulf of Mexico with no clear boundaries. This is important because international law gives countries the right to any resources found in the sea with 200 miles of their territory. When the boundaries overlap, the nations must establish an agreement as it relates to ownership of the mineral rights either by a treaty, joint development zone, joint petroleum development agreement, etc.

---

[130] Picture indicates the Western and Eastern gap of the Gulf of Mexico, retrieved from www.offshore-mag.com (Screenshot).

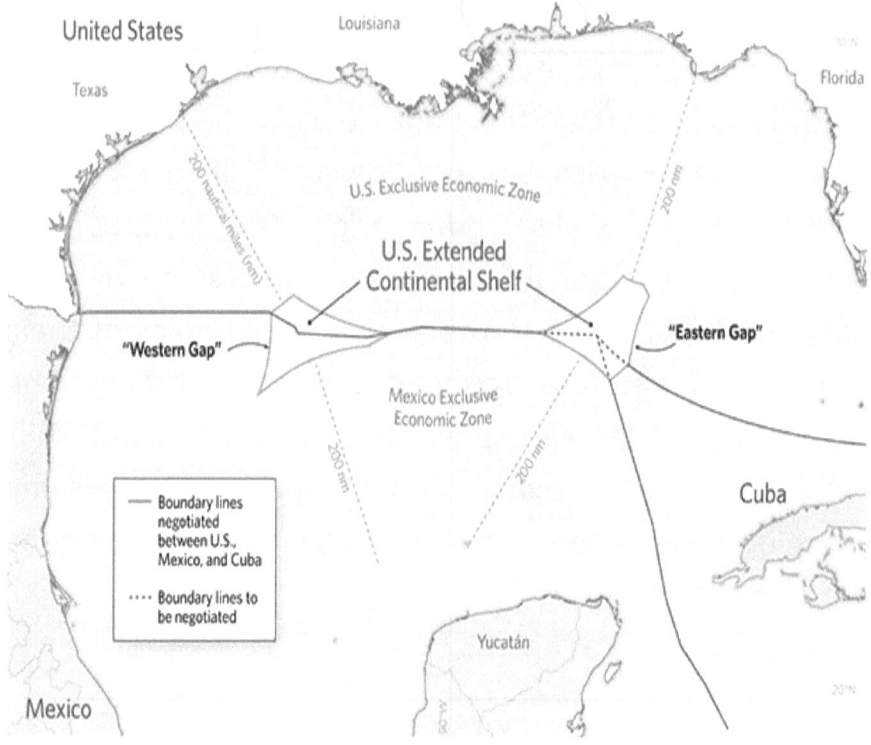

Figure 2 *Eastern Polygon that the U.S., Cuba, and Mexico overlap Exclusive Economic Zone.*

From a political perspective moderated by Mark P. Jones, Ph.D., Fellow in Political Science, Baker Institute themed, "The Not So Distant Neighbors: A Political Overview," Cristina Escobar Domínguez,[131] Lee Ann Evans, Senior Policy Advisor with Engage Cuba[132] and

---

[131] Feinberg... p. 177. Journalist, Reporter, and Anchor with the Cuban Institute of Radio and Television, Cuba. In the book, she is listed as a rising star in Millennial Voices of Cuba. Seizing an opportunity at a White House press briefing in spring 2015, she slyly inquired whether President Obama would be inclined to visit the island neighbor in light of the thawing of relations.

[132] www.engagecuba.org Engage Cuba is a national coalition of private companies, organizations, and local leaders dedicated to the advancing federal

Kerry T. Scarlott, a partner at Baker Hostetler. The panelist engaged in useful debate regarding what is viewed as the laborious and painstaking approval permit and licensing processes in Cuba.

The attendees voiced concerns and frustrations about the perceived overly bureaucratic and cumbersome process that sometimes even require Castro authorization.[133] In response, Ms. Domínguez retorted that the process requires patience on the part of would be investors. She went on to advise that the Cuban government has rightfully prioritized their foreign direct investment strategy, which means that their focus is on needed investment that generate sustainable growth and cross-industry development.[134] Ms. Domínguez further expounded on the Cuban opportunities in healthcare, tourism, transportation, construction, agriculture, and renewable energy. In her final enlightenment, she advised those with permitting concerns to review the United States Treasury's OFAC timelines and queues.

1.10.1.1 So What For Louisiana?

---

legislation to lift the Cuban embargo. Through educating and engaging local communities across the country, the organization focuses on reshaping the outdated national conversation on US-Cuba policy.

[133] Feinberg... p. 79.

[134] See video footage from Baker Institute website. www.bakerinstitute.org

Since the U.S. federal government first announced the new amendments to the Cuba regulations, the Lafayette International Center hosted Acadiana residents to a Louisiana-Cuba conference in Lafayette, LA on October 19, 2016.

Historically, the organizers noted that Cuba and Louisiana have been strong trading partners since before the island was a country and Louisiana was a state. Cuba was formerly the #1 rice buyer from Louisiana, but the more-than-50-year embargo put an end to that great relationship.

Lafayette International Center, the international trade division of Lafayette Consolidated Government, with the support of Lafayette Economic Development Authority (LEDA), Louisiana Economic Development (LED) and The Port of New Orleans organized and planned the conference, which was held at the Petroleum Club of Lafayette. The conferenced paneled participating experts from Cuba, Mexico, and the USA.

After meeting with Saul Newsome, Chairman, Louisiana Alliance for Cuba, New Orleans, LA, this author considers the Louisiana Cuba relationship to be a fundamental rekindling effort to develop lasting cemented ties that bind in the continued bilateral trust.

1.10.2 Modern U.S. Cuba Relations

Relative to the status quo of the past fifty years, these changes have been very significant and have dramatically expanded opportunities for U.S. companies and individuals to engage with Cuba.[135]

Yet President Obama enacted these changes without action or approval from Congress, and U.S. federal law continues to mandate the embargo. At the same time, legal and economic conditions on the Cuban side continue to pose significant barriers to entry into the Cuban market, and a number of complex issues, including expropriated property claims, have yet to be resolved.

1.10.2.1 So What For the Intellectual Property (Trademark) of American Business?

One of the most important, intangible, yet profitable, components of a company is the brand, product identity, markings, or trademark. The identity of major products develops international facial recognition. This resultant recognition is deliberate, strategic, and costly, and consequently, such investment requires protections. Imagine, if some of the famous U.S. brands or even more important, the "not-so- recognizable" brands in the U.S. are registered in Cuba by people not connected

---

[135] Propst, S. F., & Ford, T. J., (2016) Finding Authority and Taking Action: The President's Easing of Sanctions Against Cuba. International Law Quarterly, 32(3), 12. ("Propst")

or authorized by the brands. What happens when the unauthorized personnel seek trademark protection in the U.S.?

When it comes to trademark, the countries differ. With limited exceptions, the United States, unlike Cuba, is a use-based trademark system and requires trademark owners to prove that they are using their trademark in commerce before obtaining a registration.

1.10.2.2 So What For Trademarks? In Use.

The aforementioned "in use" approach works is laid out in the Corporate Counsel article dated April 22, 2016 titled, "Protecting Trademarks in Cuba: Time to Act Is Now."[136] If a person, natural or juridical, interested in filing for registration is not yet using a trademark in commerce, but intends to do so, the business can file an application based on its intent to use the mark. Under this process, Christiane Campbell and her coauthors, note that this intended, would be, or anticipatory user may have more than three years from filing to substantiate the application by declaring and proving actual use of the mark.

The article further explains that neither of these filing bases— use or intent to use—is restricted to U.S.

---

[136] Campbell, C.S., et. al., (2016) Protecting Trademarks in Cuba: Time to Act Is Now. https://www.corpcounsel.com dated April 22, 2016.

citizens. These protections are technically extended to and available to Cuban citizens or companies as well. This technical hurdle comes by way of the current embargo which would render it impossible for a Cuban company to demonstrate use of its mark in the United States sufficient to file based on actual use. Here is the caveat, both nations are party to a number of international conventions, including the Madrid Protocol, which allows a foreign trademark owner to extend protection of its base foreign application or registration into the United States and other countries.[137] The U.S. Patent and Trademark Office ("USPTO") reviews and accepts registration applications that have been extended through the Madrid system without requiring the mark to be first used in the United States. Therefore, an unauthorized Cuban trademark owners could extend trademark protection of a pirated or bootlegged brand in the U.S. without proving use.[138]

1.10.3 What were some underlying causes for the Obama Administration's Policy Shift?

With regard to the US-Cuba normalization swing, there was a few preliminary matters that were resolved by

---

[137] *Id.* This includes Cuban trademark owners whose base trademark application or registration may have been obtained in Cuba.

[138] According to Campbell and her coauthors, "It is important to note, however, that the country has strict maintenance requirements, and even if a U.S. registration is not originally obtained based on actual use, use of the mark in the United States must be declared and proven at each maintenance benchmark, beginning between the fifth and sixth anniversary from registration."

both sides as a testament of good faith in an effort to initiate the thawing. For instance, there was the much-celebrated handshake in 2013 between Obama-Raul Castro at the Nelson Mandela memorial ceremony. Obama apparently taking a cue from Mandela's life urging all to follow the former South African President's reconciliatory example. Additionally, the two met at the Summit of Americas in April 2015, where some suggest that Castro played up to Obama's ego suggesting that Castro believed that Obama was from humble beginnings and was honest. In 2012, the immediate preceding Summit of Americas, which met in Columbia, was marred by the Secret Service agents' prostitution scandal, but diplomatically, the hemispheric neighbors were frustrated with Cuba being "blackballed" and not being at the summit. Argentina's president scolded Obama for "maintaining an anachronistic blockade." Bolivia's president lectured that Obama was behaving "like a dictatorship." Bolivia, along with Nicaragua and Venezuela, said that they would not attend the hemispheric summit until Cuba was in attendance.

Another reason for the diplomatic thawing is the Pope influencing them by personally writing both Castro and Obama urging them to bring to an end their countries' half century stand-off. According to the Vatican, the first Latin American Pope further supported the rapprochement by hosting secret talks between U.S. and

Cuban Officials before the pontiff's visit to Cuba and the U.S. The next major "good faith" gesture between the two nation states was the prisoner ("spy") swap.[139] Cubans released U.S. Agency for International Development (USAID) contract worker, Alan Gross being held for allegedly spying and 53 other political prisoners, while in turn the U.S. released the Cuban Five (actually three now who were convicted of spying in Miami against anti-castristas along with others.[140] A.D. Winters met with Alan Gross's Cuban legal team (local counsel) and gathered that this freeing was more political posturing than a justiciable resolution.

According to Feinberg, another rationale for the historic shift is the stars had finally aligned for this sea change.[141] He goes on to explain that Cuba was facing a weak economy; the island appeared genuinely interested in stronger U.S. relations; and the Obama administration was well positioned to decisively engage the island nation. The motivations behind engagement was mutual and more than a prisoner swap, i.e., both nations acknowledged the significance of renewal diplomatic relations, the importance of a bilateral atmosphere toward the principles of international law,[142] and undoubtedly, a safer and more secure region.

---

[139] Feinberg... p. 1.
[140] Feinberg... p. 3.
[141] Feinberg... p. 2.
[142] Feinberg... p. 3.

In Obama's second term, with no more elections to campaign, he could focus on his legacy and Cuba fit within that broader theme of foreign policy similar to the nonproliferation accords with Iran. From a diplomatic standpoint, the White House decisions may be even further layered with factors that include 1) international diplomacy, 2) changes under way within the Cuba (and U.S. perceptions thereof), and 3) shifts in U.S. domestic politics.[143]

1.10.4 Obama's Actions

So what, now what? What was Cuba and the U.S. going to do of any substance to further the diplomatic thawing besides swapping spies and speeches? Well, in August 2015, Secretary Kerry raised the U.S. flag in front of the U.S. Embassy in Havana while a similar ceremony played out in Washington, D.C. earlier in the summer.[144] This is not just symbolic appointment and recognition of respective Chiefs of the Missions require each nations' President to acknowledge and authorize the diplomatic activities of the foreign Ambassador and their team. Additionally, the U.S. removed Cuba from its list of state-sponsored terrorist. The U.S. did away with the cap on remittances altogether, so there was no longer a limit on

---

[143] Feinberg... p. 4.
[144] Feinberg... p. 12.

the amount of cash a U.S. individual could carry and give to not only their family members but also for humanitarian aid projects or to spur private businesses (excluding Cuban government officials or Cuban Communist Party Officials).

Additionally, the U.S. executive branch initiated very promising regulations affecting travel and commerce by announcing revisions to the Cuban Assets Control Regulations (CACR) and Export Administration Regulation (EAR), which were designed to make travel easier by authorizing regular commercial airlines, cruise ships, ferries, and yachts to travel to Cuba.[145] The U.S. Treasury's Office of Foreign Assets Control would no longer require U.S. travelers to Cuba to apply for a license to travel. Now, travelers who fell within the permissible non-tourist categories[146] could self-validate by a simple box check.

To further illustrate its willingness to normalize relations with Cuba, on March 20, 2016, President Obama visited

---

[145] Feinberg… p. 12.

[146] The 12 authorized categories cover a wide range of possible activities: 1) Family Visits 2)Official Business of the U.S. Government, Foreign Governments, and Certain Intergovernmental Organizations, 3) Journalistic Activity 4) Professional Research, 5) Educational Activities 6) Religious Activities 7)Public Performances, Clinics, Workshops, Athletic and Other Competitions, and Exhibitions 8)Support for the Cuban People 9) Humanitarian Projects 10) Activities of Private Foundations, Research, or Educational Institutes 11) Exportation, Importation, or Transmission of Information or Information Materials 12) Certain Authorized Export Transactions.

Cuba as the first U.S. President to visit the island for an official state visit.[147] Additionally, direct mail service was restored between the two nations for the first time in 53 years. The two nations jointly approved Starwood Hotels and Resorts to refurbish and manage (but not own) two hotels in Havana.[148] The POTUS schedule was designed to promote more fluid movements of people, goods, and ideas across the Florida straits, so much so that he even engaged in a bit of sports diplomacy where the Tampa Bay Rays defeated the Cuban National Team 4-1.

While this paints an incredibly rosy picture, most U.S. business executives visiting Cuba have departed empty-handed discouraged either by many Cuban government imposed obstacles to commerce that the encountered on the island.[149] Investors in Cuba face a maze of difficulties.[150] The roadblocks presenting impediments to Cuba- U.S. economic change are largely based on bureaucratic, ideological, and legal framework. U.S products having to ultimately pass through some Cuban state trading firms which could leave U.S. firms susceptible to violating the Helms-Burton act if the businesses couldn't guarantee that the end-users were the private sector. Another significant hurdle was the financing and banking and lack of commercial credit

---

[147] Feinberg... p. 16.
[148] Feinberg... p. 17.
[149] Feinberg... p. 19.
[150] Suchlicki... p. 14.

availability.[151] American financial intermediaries demand further clarification on what transactions are permitted to be supported with commercial credits.

1.10.5 Under What Authority, Does Obama (and now Trump) Enact Easing Regulations?

Notwithstanding the framework of successive federal statutes mandating sanctions against Cuba, the President maintains broad authority and discretion to significantly ease specific provisions of the Cuba sanctions regime in support of particular U.S. foreign policy objectives recognized by Congress, including the provision of humanitarian support for the Cuban people and the promotion of democratic reforms. This executive authority to modify the Cuba sanctions is grounded in constitutional, statutory and regulatory provisions that empower the president and the responsible executive branch agencies to grant exceptions to the sanctions through executive actions, regulations and licenses.

Likewise, the U.S. Supreme Court (citing a then Congressman John Marshall speech) stated that the President is the sole organ of foreign relations and his powers are exclusive in his international exertion of legislative power. Additionally, Article II, Section 2 of

---

[151] Typically, international trade moves on credit and the cash-strapped Cuban economy was especially in need of payment assistance.

the United States Constitution, which vests broad powers in the president to conduct the foreign affairs of the United States.

These easing regulations are further supported by Section 602(a) of the Foreign Assistance Act of 1961 and Section 5(b) of the Trading with the Enemy Act (which was the statutory authority for the CACR), which grant broad authority and discretion to the president to establish and make changes to embargoes established thereunder. Pursuant to Sections 2 and 3 of Helms-Burton, President Obama has authority to provide easing measures, which reaffirm the objective of providing support for the Cuban people. Section 102(h) of Helms-Burton, which codified the CACR as it existed in March 1996, including the authority of the Secretary of Treasury to exercise licensing authority.

Some skeptics argue that U.S. business licenses are not happening in Cuba because of cronyism. General Raúl Castro introduced limited economic reforms to muddle through a difficult situation.[152] According to Jaime Suchlicki, "Yet the reforms are not structurally profound, nor are they propelling Cuba toward a free market. She writes, that economic decisions in Cuba, are determined by political and ideological considerations. The changes introduced by General Castro are not liberalizing foreign

---

[152] Suchlicki... p. 14.

investment regulations, as most Cubans cannot partner with foreign investors. From Suchlicki's perspective, "Investments in Cuba are only allowed with joint ventures ultimately controlled by military leaders or in partnerships with Grupo Gaesa.[153]

These include the inability of bureaucrats to make decisions at the local level. Fearful of making mistakes, they tend to seek permission from higher authorities. Widespread corruption and cronyism make it difficult to navigate the island's investment requirements. These are not the only problems U.S. investors will face after the embargo is terminated. A corrupt and government-controlled legal system, where judges and lawyers are appointed by the state, will complicate legal transactions and limit access to courts to litigate commercial issues.[154]

All is not awash, some non-U.S. businesses have been doing business in Cuba since the 1990's. For example, Spain has more than 250 Spanish firms operating in Cuba, with an estimated bilateral trade of $1.07 billion per year.[155] Another example is Canada, which conducts business in the areas of pharmaceuticals, mining and

---

[153] A large military group of state businesses directed by General Castro's son-in-law, General Luis Alberto López Calleja.
[154] Suchlicki… p. 14.
[155] Meyer, J. M., & Falzoni, S., (2016) The Embargo and Beyond: Legal Hurdles to Doing Business in Cuba. International Law Quarterly, 32(3), 16. ("Meyer")

hotels in Cuba. Finally, Brazil has been another player that has invested in Cuba: Brazil's investment in the Mariel port project amounted to almost $700 million.[156]

Conversely, some U.S. businesses with a much lighter footprint in the information, communications, and technology sector found entering the Cuban economy less obstructive. A prime example is Airbnb, the online rental service, where the lodging service could rapidly sign up 2,000 preexisting B&B businesses for inclusion in its list of local hosts.[157] Likewise, Verizon and Sprint, both U.S. telecommunication companies, offer long-distance calling in Cuba.[158] Even Sony Music has inked a deal giving rights to distribute some Cuban music.

As it relates to equity investments from the U.S., Rodrigo Malmierca, the Cuban minister of foreign trade and investment, cautiously instructed, "We won't keep out American business people, they are welcome, but we want to keep our relations diverse. We don't want to be tributary to anyone." This spirit of independence is telling of the attitudes and skepticism of potential trepidation by the Cuban government and people.

---

[156] Meyer... p. 16.
[157] Feinberg... p. 15.
[158] Alonso, B. P., (2016) Technology in Cuba. International Law Quarterly, 32(3), 28. Access to modern ICT services would offer benefits to the Cuban population, including: (1) improved flow of economic and market information; (2) creation of channels of communication to avert humanitarian disasters; (3) greater use of e-commerce/use of payment systems; and (4) expanded access to credit, through mobile banking applications, for example.

Author Richard Feinberg states it best when he warns that U.S. citizens and policymakers shouldn't believe "that they are the only sun in Cuba's universe." He goes on to outline how Cuba has forged diverse trading partnerships since the burn-out of its longtime benefactor the Soviet Union to include China, Brazil, Mexico, Venezuela, Europe, Canada, and UK.[159]

Critics of this vibrant international trade expansion are likely to cite Cuba's inability to generate exports required to balance trading relationships; Cuban commerce with emerging markets peaking at $8 billion in 2008; and emerging markets growing weary with continuing to extend credits to Cuba and their inability to pay.[160] A clear example of this is Cuba constantly renegotiating and restructuring its debt with Mexico, Japan, and Russia with reductions of 70-90% in exchange for extended payment plans it could meet.[161]

1.11. Cuba's Economic Lessons Learned

1.11.1 The Special Period and Beyond

Some critics of the optimistic outlook believe Cuban revolution caused several lasting residual debilities. The country was left with an underutilized, talented,

---

[159] Feinberg... p. 45.
[160] Feinberg... p. 20.
[161] As reported in Reuters quoting the Economic Intelligence Unit, who stated Cuba's total foreign debt is approximately $26B. Article Cub and the Paris Club members agree on debt total: $15B by Mark Frank.

abundance of "human capital." Additionally, the nation was left with an underperforming Cuban economy with no significant industrial or agricultural growth; further characterized by insufficient savings, sluggish exports, and chronic deficits in merchandise trade. The communist regime was nearly crippled by the collapse of the Soviet Union. This errored bet meant no more $4B in subsidies per year from the U.S.S.R that Castro had received from 1986-1990, which was 15% of Cuba's GDP. As a result, the Cuban economy took a 35% nosedive in the early 90s commonly referred to as the "periodo especial."[162]

During the special period, the Cuban government, who formerly heavily depended on Soviet subsidization of its oil deficits needs, now needed a new lifeline and in comes Venezuela and Hugo Chavez, who ascended to power in 1998 just in time. As Chavez idolized Castro (hence Venezuela's expropriation of the oil industry), he was more than happy to develop in ingenious bargaining pact. In return for Cuba sending professionals[163] (listed as services) to Venezuela and bartered goods, Cuba would receive 100,000 barrels of oil per day to 60% had to be paid for within 90 days and 40% remainder is paid

---

[162] English translation "Special Period."
[163] Many refer to this bartering system as "Doctors for Oil."

within 25 years.[164]

After the collapse of petroleum prices in conjunction with speculated economic mismanagement under Chavez and his successor, Venezuela began to tighten its international petroleum subsidies. Then along came China who rapidly became the second strongest commercial partner, where in 2014 Cuba had amassed $1.3B in consumption of Chinese goods financed by government credits and guarantees; however due to falling commodities pricing China only exported $302 million from Cuba. That's a whopping $1B trade imbalance whereas in 2015, China agreed to more lenient repayment terms, which doesn't instill confidence in potential Chinese investors.

Similar to the relations with China, in reestablishing normal relations with Cuba, Mexico forgave 70% of Cuban debt. The Mexican Secretary of Finance and Public Credit (SHCP), Luís Videgaray, reported that the Mexican Government will forgive payment of 70% of Cuba's debt to Mexico, which amounted to about US$487 million, which came from a loan that the Cuban government obtained from the National Foreign Trade Bank (Bancomext) almost 15 years earlier.[165] The foreign secretaries of Mexico and Cuba announced the re-

---

[164] Feinberg... p. 51.
[165] Gutierrez, N. (2013, November 8). Cuba; Mexico: 70% of Debt Forgiven. Retrieved November 25, 2016, from http://www.loc.gov/law/

launch of relations between the two countries and the strengthening of trade, financial, and other cooperation agreements. The Secretary of Foreign Relations of Mexico, José Antonio Meade, said Mexico will maintain a high-level political dialogue with Cuba and foster a closer relationship to develop trade relations and investment.[166]

The Minister of Foreign Affairs of Cuba, Bruno Rodríguez Parrilla, stated that it is time to strengthen bilateral ties and thanked the support of Mexico for Cuba's demand for the cessation of the economic embargo imposed by the United States on the Caribbean island. The two diplomats signed eight agreements on trade and investment, extradition, legal assistance in criminal matters, tourism, higher education, the environment and natural resources, an expansion of the agreement on economic complementation, and bilateral cooperation (a Letter of Intent).[167]

So what, now what? How does Raul Castro fix the neglect? Easy, he needs to increase labor productivity. He needs to allow international competitiveness for foreign investors competing for opportunities in Cuba. Additionally, the Castro regime must fully exploit its

---

[166] Gutierrez, N. (2013, November 8). Cuba; Mexico: Relationship Re-Launched, Agreements Signed. Retrieved November 25, 2016, from http://www.loc.gov/law/
[167] *Id.*

export capacity.[168] In May 2011, the Castro-led government initiated 313 initiatives aimed at addressing the extraordinary imbalance. One of the more promising measures was an amendment to Law 65, on November 2, 2011, the Cuban government would allow citizens who live in Cuba and foreigners, who are permanent residents, to buy and sell homes. Home ownership is limited to one primary home and one secondary home in a vacation area per individual.[169]

Irrespective of the number of measures, it is extremely challenging to motivate a workforce to work in the tobacco and sugar fields if your income is $30 or less.[170] What can incentivize young workers to produce when they can be entrepreneurs and guides for American groups like "Engage Cuba," where they can get $20 in tips and gratuity per person for 2 hour guided groups of ten, i.e., $200 for 2 hours? Or opening a restaurant in your home or turning your home into a bed and breakfast generating a decade of government income in a week. The motivation is simply not there.

In one workforce case study with Melia International Hotels, a Spanish firm who is among the leaders in the

---

[168] Feinberg... p. 25.
[169] Guerra, G. (2011, December 1). Cuba: Government Amends Housing Law to Allow Sales and Purchases of Homes. Retrieved November 25, 2016, from http://www.loc.gov/law/
[170] Feinberg... p. 27. In 2014, the Median monthly income in Cuba was 584 Cuban pesos approximately $24.33 per month.

hospitality industry, operates 28 properties in joint ventures ('JV") with the Cuban government in a management services contract to manage hotel properties on Cuba.[171] Melia finds the Cuban workforce educated and well trained. The study finds that Cubans flock to employment in the tourist industry, where they hope to gain access to tourist dollars, whether via hard currency bonuses from their employers or tips from generous tourists.[172] As pointed out in "Cuba's Secret Side" a 2-part documentary on PBS International directed by award-winning author and filmmaker, Karin Muller, even doctors and lawyers are leaving those jobs to work at the resorts versus their $27.33 monthly government salary.[173]

The so-called acceleration measures don't seem to be enough to counter the imbalance of the Cuban economic woes. These measures include extending a warmer welcome to international investments in hotels and allow foreign firms to hold equity as joint venture enterprises. In addition, the measures encouraged foreign enterprises to contract local services like I.T. and construction to local firms. As it relates to retail, the measures instituted a "local first" retail space allocation.

---

[171] Feinberg... pp. 108-109. Melia earns management fees that include a "basic fee" and an "incentive fee" based on performance.
[172] Feinberg... p. 111.
[173] Muller, K. (2013). Cuba's Secret Side. Retrieved November 25, 2016, from http://pbsinternational.org/about/

The measures went so far that it even increased ticket prices for performing arts so that the artists and singers could get paid a more attractive wage. None of this seems to be enough to calm the fears of asset protection of would be foreign investors.

1.11.2 Take It or Leave It Valuation?

In 2009, Sherritt saw a production sharing contract terminated that was signed in 1993 and is scheduled to expire in 2018, with Pebercan Inc., Sherritt's Montreal based partner. Some experts say the Cuban government prematurely terminated the agreement because CUPET, the Cuban state owned enterprise (SOE) had fell seriously behind in its scheduled payments and disputes over cost deductions. Pebercan's Cuban unit, Peberco, will get a total net lump sum payment of $140-million (U.S.) for the scrapping of the contract.

Pebercan said that Cuban authorities, through state-owned oil company Cubapetroleo SA, notified Peberco it would scrap the production sharing contract. No reason for the move was given for the Cuban move. Sherritt International (Cuba) Oil and Gas, a unit of Toronto-based Sherritt International Corp., would receive about $74-million of the $140-million payment.[174] Some critics argue that this settlement was coercive to the foreign

---

[174] Feinberg... p. 103.

investor and sends a chilling effect of any would be foreign investors. The skeptics of the deal instruct that since some compensation was offered and accepted, however grudgingly, Cuba escapes accusations of expropriation. While the equity of the lump-sum is difficult to evaluate, it illustrates a pattern to future foreign investors that if you fall out of favor with the Cuban government or if the SOE falls into arrears, then the government can choose to shut down your business and wrap the debt into a broader deal liquidating all assets. What kind of impact does this information have on potential foreign investors?

1.12. The BIT from the U.S. Perspective

1.12.1 U.S. Federal Arbitration Agreement

The U.S. has a national presumption in support of arbitration because of the consensual nature of the agreement. The United States Arbitration Act (Pub. L. 68–401, 43 Stat. 883, enacted February 12, 1925, codified at 9 U.S.C. § 1 et seq.), more commonly referred to as the Federal Arbitration Act or (" FAA"), is an act of Congress that provides for judicial facilitation of private dispute resolution through arbitration. The U.S. supreme court ruled that it applies in both state courts and federal courts, as was held constitutional in *Southland Corp. v. Keating*, 465 U.S. 1 (1984). It applies where the transaction contemplated by the parties "involves" interstate commerce and is predicated on an exercise of the Commerce Clause powers granted to Congress in the U.S. Constitution.

The FAA provides for contractually-based compulsory and binding arbitration, resulting in an arbitration award entered by an arbitrator or arbitration panel as opposed to a judgment entered by a court of law. In an arbitration, the parties give up the right to an appeal on substantive grounds to a court.

1.12.2 Texas State Arbitration Agreement

The interstate commerce test is far-reaching. However, there are cases in which courts have decided that the Texas General Arbitration Act (TGAA) controlled the agreement. The acts have many similarities and some differences. The TGAA includes considerably more detail than the FAA in its coverage of arbitration agreements, the arbitration process itself, and related proceedings, including those to compel or stay arbitration and to confirm, vacate, modify, or correct an award. Both acts require a writing or written provision for an arbitration agreement.[175] Both make an arbitration agreement valid, irrevocable and enforceable except on grounds at law or in equity for revocation of an ordinary contract.

---

[175] Grubbs, J. K., & Elliott- Howard, F. E., (2002) Texas General Arbitration Act vs. Federal Arbitration Act: Choice or Dilemma for Texas for Texas Employers? Southern Law Journal, Vol. 12, 93.

The courts follow the same analysis under both acts in determining arbitrability of an agreement: (1) whether there is an arbitration agreement and if so, (2) whether the claims between the parties come with the scope of the agreement. State contract laws are applied under both acts in each of the determinations. The courts are guided by the same strong federal and State of Texas presumptions favoring arbitration in analyses under both acts.

According to the UNCTD, the U.S. has 46 BITS and 67 Treaties with Investment provisions.[176]

---

[176] http://investmentpolicyhub.unctad.org/IIA/CountryOtherIias/223#iiaInnerMenu

U.S.
Bilateral Investment Treaties

No.	Title (short)	Status	Date of signature	Date of entry into force
1	Albania - United States of America BIT	In force	11/01/1995	04/01/1998
2	Argentina - United States of America	In force	14/11/1991	20/10/1994
3	Armenia - United States of America BIT	In force	23/09/1992	29/03/1996
4	Azerbaijan - United States of America	In force	01/08/1997	02/08/2001
5	Bahrain - United States of America BIT	In force	29/09/1999	30/05/2001
6	Bangladesh - United States of America	In force	12/03/1986	25/07/1989
7	Belarus - United States of America BIT	Signed	15/01/1994	
8	Bolivia, Plurinational State of - United	Terminated	17/04/1998	06/06/2001
9	Bulgaria - United States of America BIT	In force	23/09/1992	02/06/1994
10	Cameroon - United States of America	In force	26/02/1986	06/04/1989
11	Congo, Democratic Republic of the -	In force	03/08/1984	28/07/1989
12	Congo - United States of America BIT	In force	12/02/1990	13/08/1994
13	Croatia - United States of America BIT	In force	13/07/1996	20/06/2001
14	Czech Republic - United States of	In force	22/10/1991	19/12/1992
15	Ecuador - United States of America BIT	Terminated	27/08/1993	11/05/1997
16	Egypt - United States of America BIT	In force	11/03/1986	27/06/1992
17	El Salvador - United States of America	Signed	10/03/1999	
18	Estonia - United States of America BIT	In force	19/04/1994	16/02/1997
19	Georgia - United States of America BIT	In force	07/03/1994	10/08/1999
20	Grenada - United States of America BIT	In force	02/05/1986	03/03/1989
21	Haiti - United States of America BIT	Signed	13/12/1983	
22	Honduras - United States of America	In force	01/07/1995	11/07/2001
23	Jamaica - United States of America BIT	In force	04/02/1994	07/03/1997
24	Jordan - United States of America BIT	In force	02/07/1997	12/06/2003
25	Kazakhstan - United States of America	In force	19/05/1992	12/01/1994
26	Kyrgyzstan - United States of America	In force	19/01/1993	12/01/1994
27	Latvia - United States of America BIT	In force	13/01/1995	26/12/1996
28	Lithuania - United States of America	In force	14/01/1998	13/06/2004
29	Moldova, Republic of - United States of	In force	21/04/1993	26/11/1994
30	Mongolia - United States of America	In force	06/10/1994	04/01/1997

U.S.
Bilateral Investment Treaties

31	Morocco - United States of America	In force	22/07/1985	29/05/1991
32	Mozambique - United States of	In force	01/12/1998	03/03/2005
33	Nicaragua - United States of America	Signed	01/07/1995	
34	Panama - United States of America BIT	In force	27/10/1982	30/05/1991
35	Poland - United States of America BIT	In force	21/03/1990	06/08/1994
36	Romania - United States of America BIT	In force	28/05/1992	15/01/1994
37	Russian Federation - United States of	Signed	17/06/1992	
38	Rwanda - United States of America BIT	In force	19/02/2008	01/01/2012
39	Senegal - United States of America BIT	In force	06/12/1983	25/10/1990
40	Slovakia - United States of America BIT	In force	22/10/1991	19/12/1992
41	Sri Lanka - United States of America	In force	20/09/1991	01/05/1993
42	Trinidad and Tobago - United States of	In force	26/09/1994	26/12/1996
43	Tunisia - United States of America BIT	In force	15/05/1990	07/02/1993
44	Turkey - United States of America BIT	In force	03/12/1985	18/05/1990
45	Ukraine - United States of America BIT	In force	04/03/1994	16/11/1996
46	United States of America - Uruguay BIT	In force	04/11/2005	31/10/2006
47	United States of America - Uzbekistan	Signed	16/12/1994	

1.12.3 U.S. BIT Litigation

An example of U.S. state-state and investor-state dispute that Cuba should be keenly aware in its potential BIT negotiations with the U.S. would be Ecuador v. United States, which began after Ecuador disagreed with the *Chevron v. Ecuador*[177] Tribunal's interpretation

---

[177] *Chevron Corp. (U.S.) v. Ecuador*, PCA Case No. 34877, Partial Award on the Merits, ¶¶ 242–44(Perm. Ct. Arb. 2010) [hereinafter Chevron v. Ecuador]

about whether the U.S.-Ecuador BIT's "effective means" clause created an obligation equal to or more demanding than customary international law. This was a convoluted case discussed in Julian Cardenas' Transnational Investment Law class. This was triggered in the Ecuadorian national courts, where a suit alleged that from 1964 to 1990, Chevron contaminated the Amazon rainforest when it operated a consortium which included Ecuador's state-owned oil company, Petroecuador. According to reports a court-appointed expert estimated the potential damages for cleanup and illnesses at $27 billion.

A group of Ecuadorean indigenous people initially sued Texaco, which is now owned by Chevron, in a New York federal district court in 1993. The suit alleged the company polluted the rainforest and rivers, causing environmental damage and personal injuries as a result of its business. Chevron then requested that the case be resolved in an Ecuadorian court, and it was refiled in Lago Agrio, Ecuador. Then Chevron claimed that due to political pressures on the judiciaries, the company wouldn't receive a fair trial in Ecuadorian courts. Chevron sought arbitration in the Permanent Court of Arbitration in The Hague.[178]

Pursuant to the BIT, Ecuador sought an interpretive

---

[178] *Chevron v. Ecuador*, PCA Case No. 34877

agreement on the point, but the United States refused to respond. Ecuador then launched a state-to-state arbitration seeking an interpretation, to which the United States objected on the basis that there was no concrete dispute between the parties. The Tribunal's award has not been publicly released, but the majority reportedly dismissed the claim because (1) there was no concrete dispute with practical consequences between Ecuador and the United States, as opposed to between Ecuador and U.S. investors; and (2) there was no dispute because the United States, by remaining silent, had not put itself in "positive opposition" to Ecuador's interpretation. Ultimately, the U.S. State Department's inaction and silence was a clever way to protect its home state private entity, which consequently happened to be the second largest U.S. oil company.

1.13. Best Practices in BIT Establishment

In sum, these two nations have to engage in joint diplomacy in scene setting for business protection and bilateral investment treaty network development. First, each must grant each other preferential treatment in the investment protection articles guaranteeing freedom from arbitrary taking, e.g., "most favored nation or national treatment." Second, the two states must provide a very liberal policy for independent dispute resolution i.e., commercial arbitration which includes interim measures to freeze assets. Thirdly, these two neighbors must offer investors the right to transfer funds without delay using market rates of exchange. Finally, in order to develop the atmospheric conditions for contracting a bilateral investment treaty between the U.S. and Cuba, they must ensure the senior management selection and freedom from unreasonable inefficiency rules that infringe on competitiveness absent health, security, safety, and environmental exceptions.

1.14. Conclusion

Bottom line, both the governments and the citizens, whether juridical or natural, in the United States and Cuba need to exhibit patience, understanding, respect, and continued engagement. First, from a patience standpoint, the U.S. needs only to look to the complicated history that Cuba has endured to have a right of self-determination from Spanish imperialism; U.S. protectorate (occupation); constant instability of westernized puppets; Castro-led Soviet-funded brutality; to an insolvency dictated by a U.S.-led embargo; constant external regime change attempts; to voila - open for business? On the other hand, the Cuban people and Raul regime (now that Fidel has died) must exhibit tolerance with U.S. cautious optimism and trepidation with entering Cuba. After all, it was the Castro regime that has engaged in serious human rights violation with the "El Paredon" dissident eradications; the $1.8 billion-dollar expropriation of U.S. owned property (roughly worth $7 billion in today's terms with a 6% interest); to allowing the Soviet's to place nuclear weapons 90 nautical miles from the U.S. mainland.

Next, each nation's governments, corporate opportunists, and regular citizens (presumably Jose Q. Publico and John Q. Public) need to display understanding of these complication, for this complex history will shape any new bilateral investments that are not equivocated by embargos and threat of uncompensated nationalization. The understanding has to be deep and altruistic in viewing the other nation's actions leading up to any potential treaties with optical optimism and lenses of best intentions.

Then, these hemispheric neighbors are required to show mutual respect towards each other's sovereignty. More than mere empty rhetorical language of admiration, but real, internationally recognized respect of the other right to create and make laws that it sees sufficient in government irrespective of the other nation's principled objections or business inconveniences. Both Cuba and the U.S. must respect each other enough to restrain from enacting laws or executive regulations have extraterritorial reach. Both countries' parliamentary bodies must practice respect for the people of the opposite citizens by not creating laws that are neither unduly harsh towards specifically the opposite business interest which manifestly discriminates against or singles out the neighbor's citizens. Ultimately, the U.S. must lift the universally-recognized as useless embargo (called a blockade by Cubans) and pay back rent at fair-market value for the naval base at Guantanamo Bay. The Cuban government must fully recognize commercial arbitrations and submit in certain cases to their adjudication as an independent alternative for foreign business investment dispute resolution as opposed to constant debt-restructuring. Lastly, Cuba is required to pay the fair market value of the confiscated American property and fund the settlement of the expropriation minus the amount that has been seized by the U.S. government.

Finally, the U.S. and Cuba must commit to consistent and cautiously optimistic policy of engagement. This U.S. led engagement has to find an equilibrium, maybe not to the level of the overly optimistic hurriedly, business oriented level of Engage Cuba, but definitely not to the overly pessimistic anticastritas of south Florida's CANF. The newly-elected Trump State Department has to use tried and true sound diplomatic negotiations and statecraft (non-Twitter®) in furtherance of such engagement. Conversely, Cuba, with its potential equal-footing, Napeleonic complex, has to get over its egotistical hand-wrenching, vacillating, and recognize that engaging the world's largest economy (330 million potential customers minus the 2 million disenchanted south Floridians) may present some benefits to the government and citizens alike in technological advancements, industrial progressions, banking access, and infrastructural improvement not to mention the ambit of protection that comes along the American military. Not to mention allowing Cuba to exploit the American medical markets with their robust medically proficient workforce. So what, now what? This infancy "normalization" mandates patience by both in some areas; however, in touch points that are mutually beneficial, the states are obliged to fully exploit this multi-national relationship from hemispheric economics; regional security; generally accepted international customs; and most importantly from each nation's sovereign interest.

CHAPTER 2: ALL AROUND THE WORLD, SAME SONG!

A Comparative Civil Rights Analysis Between the U.S., Latin America, and Cuba.

The borrowed Digital Underground song title is apropos when comparing multinational civil rights. Whether the nations under evaluation are the United States, the Latin American region, or the island neighbor of Cuba, these rights must be viewed as international human rights. The development of these rights tends to grow with national progress, while ebbing and flowing with new globally accepted norms.

In some instances, however, the Courts have stood up and moved the countries forward by redefining civil liberties for modern circumstances. While ignorance, hatred, fearmongering, and bigotry ruled initial evaluations of civil freedoms, thoughtful, deliberate, and profound legal analysis has begun to carry the day. Thus, this comparative study focuses on equal protection structure under the law; religious freedoms and "freedom from" thereof; and the progression of LGBTI movement.

2.0 INTRODUCTION

At the outset, this segment of the book aims to compare human rights development between the U.S. and Cuba relating to the Latin American model. The author acknowledges that taking on the task is humongous as if an ant eating an elephant, but the best way for an ant to eat an elephant is "one bite at a time." Thus, this comparative study will choose selective meaty bite-sized portions of the overall analysis and focus on equal protection structure under the law; religious freedoms and "freedom from" thereof; and the progression of LGBTI movement. The article uses numerous sources but will heavily cite the Latin American casebook. As a warning, the author acknowledges limits to the accessibility to primary verifiable Cuban sources but he has cross-referenced dual cites for vetting purposes.

Since the researcher's emphasis compares multiple nations, shaping an understanding of international law would prove useful. According to Professor Paust, there are two basic types of international law: (1) international agreements, and (2) customary international law.[179] First, international agreements come in forms of

---

[179] Paust, Jordan J., M. Cheriff Bassiouni, and Michael P. Scharf. Human Rights Module on Crimes Against Humanity, Genocide, Other Crimes Against Human Rights, and War Crimes Third Edition. N.p.: Carolina Academic Press, 2013. p. 3.

treaties, conventions, protocol, etc., but are binding only on the parties to the agreement, their citizens, or possibly those with a significant nexus with one of the contracting parties. Generally, these contracts will have treatment clauses like "most favored nations treaty," "fair and equitable treatment," or "national treatment." These provisions are designed to foster equal economic protection between two nation states and citizens doing business in a foreign state.

Paust then describes customary law as a "dynamic process of behavior and expectations."[180] It is important to note that universality or unanimity are not required for customs instead they need to be generally shared in the international community. Likewise, Article 38 of the advisory opinion wielding International Court of Justice ("I.C.J.")[181] defines the term as the "general practice accepted as law." Two other higher-level categories of international law are **1)** *obligatio erga omnes* and **2)** *jus cogens*. *Obligatio erga omnes* are obligations to all humankind. The term *jus cogens* involves customary peremptory norms that preempt any other inconsistent international law, i.e., torture, forced disappearance of persons, slavery, genocide, systematic racial

---

[180] *Id.* at 4.
[181] ICJ's competence is generally involves advisory opinions at the request certain U.N. entities or controversies arising between states.

discrimination and more.[182] The above concepts provide guidance as the book explores the similarities and differences of rights in the U.S., Cuba, and Latin America.

2.1 Equal Protection

From an international perspective, the Universal Declaration of Human Rights ("UDHR") contains two different categories of human rights – civil and political rights on one side; and economic, social, and cultural rights on the other.[183] Civil and political rights include the rights to life, free expression, freedom of religion, fair trial, and self-determination; and to be free from torture, cruel treatment, and arbitrary detention. In comparison, economic, social, and cultural rights consist of the rights to education, healthcare, social security, unemployment insurance, paid maternity leave, equal pay for equal work, reduction of infant mortality; prevention, treatment, and control of diseases; and to form and join unions and strike.

The initial chomp of the elephant-sized task involves the comparison of equal protection of the U.S., Latin America, and Cuba. First, what is equal protection in America? According to Cornell Law's Legal Information

---

[182] *Paust* at 5.
[183] "Universal Declaration of Human Rights." *United Nations*. United Nations, n.d. Web. 26 Apr. 2017. http://www.un.org/en/universal-declaration-human-rights/. The Universal Declaration of Human Rights (UDHR) is a milestone document in the history of human rights.

Institute ("LII"), the U.S. Constitution prohibits states from denying any person within its territory the equal protection of the laws. In other words, a state must treat an individual in the same manner as others similarly situated. The Fourteenth amendment's equal protection clause forces a state to govern impartially— not draw distinctions between individuals solely on differences that are irrelevant to a legitimate governmental objective.[184] Thus, the equal protection clause provides the sword of justice designed to slash civil rights offenders.

2.2 Equality in the U.S.

Early in the founding of the republic, equal protection grew to become synonymous with "equality of opportunity" and largely recognized as vital to the American experience. From the beginning, Americans believed that the "New World" differed from Europe -- where a man's destiny was largely determined by his social class pursuant to caste system.[185] By contrast, the United States peddles the concept that "a man's success depends on his ability, ingenuity, and character." This marketing strategy captured in the phraseology

---

[184] Staff, LII. "Equal Protection." LII / Legal Information Institute. N.p., 06 Aug. 2007. Web. 26 Apr. 2017. https://www.law.cornell.edu/wex/equal_protection . Legal Information Institute. "Equal Protection."

[185] "Equality Of Opportunity Under Globalization: Full Chapter." Freedom House. N.p., n.d. Web. 26 Apr. 2017. https://freedomhouse.org/report/todays-american-how-free/equality-opportunity-under-globalization-full-chapter .

"American Dream" expresses the ideal that everyone possesses the potential to attain a degree of prosperity.[186] While the pitch seems great, the execution was marginalized by institutionalized unequal treatment and systematic application of discrimination.

Under the horrendous system of slavery and the subsequent atrocities of segregation, blacks were denied practically every avenue to prosperity, saving community-based black on black enterprises.[187] Until relatively recently, women and other minorities were subjected to organized inequality and even discouraged from entering certain professions and excluded from positions of authority.[188] This must be in the small print of the "American Dream" contract.

Even if the equal protection was not offered to certain segments of the pre-civil War era citizens, the 1868 modification of the constitution surely guaranteed it? Wrong! This amendment has been subject to litigation and formed a wealth of precedent to provide further clarity and future legislation to support effectuation.

According to LII, every equal protection clause issue can

---

[186] *Id.*
[187] *Id.*
[188] *Id.*

be broken down into three main questions:[189]

1. **What classification does a government action create?**
2. **What level of scrutiny should be applied to this classification?**
3. **Does this governmental action meet that scrutiny level?**

In classification, the government action can facially classify people or be facially neutral, but has a disparate impact on a particular group of people. Facially neutral classification creates a more difficult analysis, where a plaintiff must demonstrate that the government intended to discriminate against the affected group and the discrimination had an effect. If either prong is unmet, then the analysis stops.

After that, a level of scrutiny is selected to evaluate the government's classification. The more egregious the classification, the higher a level of scrutiny it would need to meet constitutional muster.[190] In the American analysis, the three standards of review are strict scrutiny,[191] intermediate scrutiny,[192] and rationale basis

---

[189] Staff, LII. "Equal Protection." LII / Legal Information Institute. N.p., 06 Aug. 2007. Web. 26 Apr. 2017. https://www.law.cornell.edu/wex/equal_protection . Legal Information Institute. "Equal Protection."
[190] *Id.*
[191] *Id.* When a law is subject to strict scrutiny, the government must prove that the law is narrowly tailored to advance a compelling government interest. This

test.[193] This modern complicated judicial system of balance and counterbalance is likely why most objective NGOs rank America high regarding equal protection of law. Yet despite the U.S. constant, frequent, and incessant failure to live up to its ideals, for many in the world the United States remains the land of opportunity simply because it is better than their former country. This sentiment is probably because of Americans, like John Marshall Harlan (half-brother of a blue-eyed high yellow slave), the "Great Dissenter" who observed the full perspective:

---

means that the classification is no broader than absolutely necessary. The government interest must be compelling enough to warrant the classification. Strict scrutiny applies whenever a law targets a "suspect class" or burdens one's right to exercise a "fundamental right." A law discriminates on basis of a "suspect class," if it classifies people on basis of race, national origin, or, in certain cases, non-U.S. citizenship (i.e. discriminates against documented aliens within the United States). Thus, a law would not be subject to strict scrutiny if it discriminates against undocumented aliens or aliens outside of the United States. A law burdens a "fundamental right" if it affects rights such as the freedom of speech, the right to marry, the right to travel, the right to vote, etc.

[192] *Id.* Intermediate Scrutiny is less rigorous than strict scrutiny. When a law is subject to intermediate scrutiny, the government has the burden of proving that the statutory classification is substantially related to a legitimate government objective. Thus, a law fails intermediate scrutiny if it does substantially advance a government objective, or if the objective is not legitimate (e.g. based on stereotype, bias, or animus). A law is subject to intermediate scrutiny if it burdens a "quasi-suspect class." A class is characterized "quasi-suspect" if the class is not entirely politically powerless, but traditionally lacks substantial political power. For example, women are considered a quasi-suspect class. Laws that burden children born out of wedlock are also subjected to intermediate scrutiny.

[193] Rational basis review is the lowest level of scrutiny, where an individual challenging the law – not the government – must prove that the classification is not reasonably related to some rational purpose. In other words, an individual must prove that the classification advances no government purpose: either by showing that the purpose is illegitimate, arbitrary, or capricious, or that the law cannot possibly advance it.

The white race deems itself to be the dominant race in this country. And so it is, in prestige, in achievements, in education, in wealth, and in power. So, I doubt not, it will continue to be for all time, if it remains true to its great heritage and holds fast to the principles of constitutional liberty. But in the view of the Constitution, in the eye of the law, there is in this country no superior, dominant, ruling class of citizens. There is no caste here. Our Constitution is color-blind and neither knows nor tolerates classes among citizens. In respect of civil rights, all citizens are equal before the law. The humblest is the peer of the most powerful. The law regards man as man and takes no account of his surroundings or of his color when his civil rights as guaranteed by the supreme law of the land are involved....

The arbitrary separation of citizens, on the basis of race, while they are on a public highway, is a badge of servitude wholly inconsistent with the civil freedom and the equality before the law established by the Constitution. It cannot be justified upon any legal grounds...

> We boast of the freedom enjoyed by our people above all other peoples. But it is difficult to reconcile that boast with the state of the law which, practically, puts the brand of servitude and degradation upon a large class of our fellow citizens, our equals before the law. The thin disguise of "equal" accommodations for passengers in railroad coaches will not mislead anyone, nor atone for the wrong this day done....

America still serves as a beacon to those in other nations who suffer poverty, repression, or both. Conversely, she still fails to shine that same light on its own citizenry in examples of state-sponsored over-policing and excessive prosecutions of black and brown persons; inter-generational denial of America's afro-descendants access to capital from financial institutions; an apathetic ambivalence toward blatant undermining of the fundamental truths of the Fourteenth amendment, among others. In forming the framer's more perfect union, consider classic examples: non-enforcement of President Lincoln and General Sherman's forty-acres proclamation; Jim Crow laws; the need for a Nineteenth amendment; *Brown v. Board of Education & Mendez v. Westminster*; Black Farmer's suit; Japanese internment camps; gender pay inequality; the Tuskegee Institute syphilis experiment;[194] the need for '60s civil rights legislation; the Helms-Burton act of the Cuban Embargo; and the *Obergefell v. Hodges* case. Now, before comparing Cuban's equal protection model, let's look at the Latin American model.

2.21 Latin American Equality

A consensus[195] reveals Latin America exhibits profound traces of social, economic, and political inequality, which can be construed in terms of redistribution, as well as a lack of recognition.[196] This inequality lingers despite public policy efforts designed to address the more severe forms of inequality. Both applying the equality

---

[194] "Tuskegee Health Benefit Program." Centers for Disease Control and Prevention. Centers for Disease Control and Prevention, 17 Apr. 2017. Web. 26 Apr. 2017. http://www.cdc.gov/. In the summer of 1973, a class-action lawsuit was filed on behalf of the study participants and their families. In 1974, a $10 million out-of-court settlement was reached. As part of the settlement, the U.S. government promised to give lifetime medical benefits and burial services to all living participants. The Tuskegee Health Benefit Program (THBP) was established to provide these services. In 1975, wives, widows and offspring were added to the program. In 1995, the program was expanded to include health as well as medical benefits. The Centers for Disease Control and Prevention was given responsibility for the program, where it remains today in the National Center for HIV/AIDS, Viral Hepatitis, STD, and TB Prevention. The last study participant died in January 2004. The last widow receiving THBP benefits died in January 2009. There are 12 offspring currently receiving medical and health benefits.

[195] F., González Bertomeu Juan, and Roberto Gargarella. The Latin American casebook: courts, constitutions and rights. Farnham, Surrey: Ashgate, 2016. Print. A large number of academic studies and reports by international human rights organizations, non-governmental organizations, and community-based organizations deliver the same diagnosis:

[196] *Id.*

principles or even the principle of non-arbitrary discrimination under strict scrutiny, have proven unsuccessful in guaranteeing actual equal conditions for the exercise of legal rights.

While the U.S. model of equality focuses on equal treatment, the Latin American principle of equality was originally designed to prevent arbitrary governmental acts. Ultimately, the Latin American model acquired a restorative function to counter inequalities, from the development of social rights to economic, social, and cultural rights.[197] Starting to mirror the American model, the principle of equality is fulfilled "as long as all individuals who are under the same circumstances are treated in the same manner."[198]

In a further comparison of the Latin American equal protection, this book shifts to how the courts dissect the application of equality. One of the more elaborate versions is the integrated test, which combines the principle of proportionality used by European case law with the American courts' approach of a higher or lower intensity of control.[199] This integrated test analyzes suitability, necessity, and proportionality. It, also, includes the intensity of control while addressing the

---

[197] *Id.*
[198] *Id.*
[199] *Id.* (scrutiny tests: mere rationality test, intermediate scrutiny test, and strict scrutiny test which applies to suspect classifications).

reasoning behind the classification. Finally, the integrated test weighs the importance of the grounds on which the challenged laws or regulations were approved. The casebook authors demand positive action and not finding the substantive legal equality as convincing enough to challenge a status quo of inequality. The authors conclude that "no form of the equality principle may be validly achieved, within a democratic context, without the involvement of those who are in actual situations of disparity."[200]

2.22 Castro Equality

Now, this chapter shifts to Cuba. In a 2016 posting, Thomas Jefferson School of Law Professor Marjorie Cohn[201] compares Cuba's human rights record with the U.S. and opines, "the U.S. should be taking lessons from Cuba." She further added, "The U.S. government criticizes civil and political rights in Cuba while disregarding Cubans' superior access to universal housing, health care, education, and its guarantee of paid maternity leave and equal pay rates." Professor Cohn attributes any atrocities in Cuba to the U.S. embargo like other writers on Cuban inequality seemingly glossing over the glaring details of inequality

---

[200] *Id.*
[201] Cohn, Marjorie. "Human Rights Hypocrisy: US Criticizes Cuba." Marjorie Cohn. N.p., n.d. Web. 26 Apr. 2017. http://marjoriecohn.com/human-rights-hypocrisy-us-criticizes-cuba/.

and unfair treatment and shoot straight to the "freebies. While this author loves freebies as much as the next human, the discussion calls for a more objective dialogue than what Ms. Cohn limits herself.

In her article, "Human Rights Hypocrisy: U.S. Criticizes Cuba," she applauds "the remarkable panoply of human rights" that the Cuban government guarantees. She appreciates the island's healthcare[202] as prevention-focused with pioneering treatments for lung cancer and diabetic amputations. Next, she commends Cuba's version of free education, which is a universal right up to and including higher education.[203] Cohn observed, "Cuba spends a larger proportion of its GDP on education than any other country in the world." The "Hypocrisy" article further extols Cuba's "promise" for a free electoral process starting in 2018 with term limits for senior officials. She even praises the labor market where Cuban lawyers earn about $25 USD per month and like many in the workforce quit and enter the tourism market.

She praises Cuba's rights on women issues. She cites that women make up the majority of judges, attorneys, scientists, public health workers and professionals. Cuban women make up 48% of the members of parliament, which is third highest in the world. In her life

---

[202] Healthcare is considered a right in Cuba. Universal healthcare is free to all. Cuba has the highest ratio of doctors to patients in the world at 6.7 per 1,000.
[203] Cohn, Marjorie.

expectancy comparison, she illustrated how Cuba was on par and often outperformed the U.S. in certain metrics.[204]

Citing a Cornell Law school study, she suggests that there is no one under sentence of death in Cuba and no one on death row in October 2015. Further adding, that in December 2010, Cuba's Supreme Court commuted the death sentence of Cuba's last remaining death row inmate and no new death sentences are known to have been imposed since that time. In contrast, a 2016 Death Penalty Information shows 2,949 people were on death row in state facilities in the United States and 62 on death row in federal lockup. At the drafting of this article, Arkansas originally set four double executions over an 11-day period in April. The U.S. Supreme Court cleared the way for the southern State to conduct a "2 for 1" execution. In a 5-4 vote, the court of last resort rejected appeals that would have halted one of the state sponsored killings.[205]

As it relates to the environment, the World Wildlife Fund ("WWF"), a leading global environmental organization, found that Cuba was the only country in the world to

---

[204] Id.
[205] "Arkansas Supreme Court clears way for state's first execution in 12 years." Fox News. FOX News Network, 20 Apr. 2017. Web. 26 Apr. 2017. http://www.foxnews.com/politics/2017/04/20/arkansas-supreme-court-clears-way-for-states-first-execution-in-12-years.html.

have achieved sustainable development. WWF report author's attributed Cuba reaching this UN's sustainability stature due to its high literacy level and a very high life expectancy, while the nation's ecological footprint is not large since it is a country with low energy consumption.[206]

Ultimately, Professor Cohn urges the U.S. to stop lecturing Cuba and lift the embargo to which she refers to "blockade." She quotes the Cuban delegation's lead, Pedro Luis Pedroso, during bilateral human rights' talks when he said, "We expressed our concerns regarding discrimination and racism patterns in U.S. society, the worsening of police brutality, torture acts and extrajudicial executions in the fight on terror and the legal limbo of prisoners at the U.S. prison camp in Guantanamo." The law professor concludes that lecturing Cuba about its human rights while denying many basic human rights to the American people is glaring.[207]

This author readily admits that most signs point to Cuba's Equal Protection progressive growth. However, and notwithstanding Professor Cohn's finger wagging, Cuba has current gaps and seams with due process. As recent as August 2018, Cuba charged Jose Daniel Ferrer

---

[206] "Colombia's Biodiversity." WWF - Find your local WWF office. N.p., n.d. Web. 26 Apr. 2017. http://www.wwf.org/.
[207] Cohn, Marjorie.

along with his colleague, Ebert Hidalgo Cruz, with attempted murder. Mr. Ferrer is the leader of Patriotic Union of Cuba ("UNPACU"), one of Cuba's largest and most active opposition organizations.

The arrest stems from a traffic accident involving a plain-clothed security official. Many reports confirm that Amnesty International and the U.S. State Department expressed concerns with Mr. Ferrer being held incommunicado in Santiago De Cuba and called for a clarification on his detention. In a tweet, State Department officials cautioned, "No family visit, no lawyer, no due process, no justice." U.S. officials went so far as to demand the two detainees' release.

2.3 Religious Freedom

The next section focuses on the challenging relationship between religion and the state. With a bit of oversimplification, the religious constitutional conflicts are generally classified into two groups: 1) freedom of religion and 2) disputes regarding freedom from religion (including freedom to have "no religion"). The distinction between cases of freedom of religion and freedom from religion should not be taken in *toto*.[208] In arguendo, the casebook's authors contemplate that

---

[208] Latin American Casebook.

when the state imposes or endorses, whether directly or indirectly, a religious practice, symbol or belief, it impacts negatively on the religious freedom of those who do not share the belief in question.[209]

In the U.S., everyone technically has the right to practice his or her own religion, or no religion at all. With varying religious views, the American forefathers believed the best way to protect religious liberty was to keep the government out of religion. Thus, the Bill of Rights commenced with the First Amendment -- to guarantee the separation of church and state.[210] The amendment is broken down further into two clauses: 1) the establishment clause and 2) the free exercise clause. The Establishment Clause of the First Amendment prohibits government from encouraging or promoting ("establishing") religion in any way. The Free Exercise Clause of the First Amendment gives you the right to worship or not as you choose. Basically, the government can't penalize you because of your religious beliefs.

Like most U.S. legal concepts, it is not quite that simple. There is a test to evaluate whether a government action is repugnant to the establishment or free exercise clauses. In 1971, the Supreme Court created three tests

---

[209] Latin American Casebook.
[210] "Your Right to Religious Freedom." American Civil Liberties Union. N.p., n.d. Web. 26 Apr. 2017. https://www.aclu.org/other/your-right-religious-freedom.

for determining whether a particular government act or policy unconstitutionally promotes religion.

The Lemon test[211] says a policy meets constitutional muster, if it:

1. **Has a non-religious purpose;**
2. **Not end up promoting or favoring any set of religious beliefs; and**
3. **Not overly involve the government with religion.**

The American constitutional conflict has a "bright line" test to allow quick evaluation of government acts. So why is there an Office of International Religious Freedom ("IRF") in the State Department that has the mission of promoting religious freedom as a core objective of U.S. foreign policy? The Ambassador-at-Large for International Religious Freedom leads this and monitors religious persecution and discrimination worldwide, recommends and implements policies in respective regions or countries, and develops programs to promote religious freedom.[212]

Illustrating the U.S. commitment to religious freedom, and to the international covenants that guarantee it as the inalienable right of every human being, the IRF seeks

---

[211] *Lemon v. Kurtzman*, 403 U.S. 602 (1971)
[212] "International Religious Freedom." U.S. Department of State. U.S. Department of State, n.d. Web. 26 Apr. 2017. https://www.state.gov/j/drl/irf/ .

to:

1. **Promote freedom of religion and conscience throughout the world as a fundamental human right and as a source of stability for all countries;**
2. **Assist emerging democracies in implementing freedom of religion and conscience;**
3. **Assist religious and human rights NGOs in promoting religious freedom;**
4. **Identify and denounce regimes that are severe persecutors on the basis of religious belief.**[213]

This office even has a list captured in the annual International Religious Freedom report.[214] Well, there went that bright line in Lemon case.

2.31 Latin American Region's Religiosity

The blurred line is even murkier in Latin America. One glaring issue is the ubiquitous role of Catholic Church and the huge influence of Catholicism as the majority religion. Historically, the Catholic Church has had a grip on and continues to be dominant in practically every Latin American country, but it is not the only religion. Nevertheless, this influence is likely to shape legislators,

---

[213] "International Religious Freedom." U.S. Department of State. U.S. Department of State, n.d. Web. 26 Apr. 2017. https://www.state.gov/j/drl/irf/.
[214] *Id.*

jurists, and executives' actions leading to active policies that support Catholic viewpoints as part of the state's "duty to maintain inter-generational bonds or to foment a society's culture and roots."[215] When a country engages in this "justified" promotion of religiosity, there is an appreciable risk of creating or reinforcing a sort of stratification of first-class and second-class citizens. Since the Latin American countries are not uniform in the evaluation of religious based conflicts, it would prove as futile an effort as ant eating the elephant to lump the many nations in one. Nonetheless, the casebook offers tools for analyzing the church-state relationship:

> a) There is a religion that historically has been, and still is, predominant in Latin America: the Catholic Church;
>
> b) This is an institution that has had, and continues to have, a strong political weight;
>
> c) Thus, identifying the degrees of separation and autonomy between the states and this church is of great importance;
>
> d) It is also important to reflect on the

---

[215] Latin American Casebook.

capacity of the state to impose its authority and its laws on that church; and, lastly,

e) It is important to consider that each state in the region shows differences in this particular area.

With that in mind, let's shift to Cuba's religiosity conflicts. Prior to the revolution, Cuba's religious foundation was a reliable bastion of Catholicism. The Roman Catholic Church estimated 90% of the population was Catholic; then came Fidel Castro. While Castro and his bearded gang of rebels established policies in favor of freedom of religion, that wasn't the case in practice.

2.32 Castro's Losing and Regaining His Religion

Once, Cuban leader Fidel Castro announced his alliance to the Stalinist regime, he adopted an adversity to anything religious. Castro's Communist Party closed churches and over 400 hundred Catholic schools; nationalized properties owned by religious organizations;[216] and forced the faithful underground.[217]

---

[216] Gomez, Alan. "Religious history complicated in communist Cuba." USA Today. Gannett Satellite Information Network, 22 Sept. 2015. Web. 26 Apr. 2017. https://www.usatoday.com/story/news/2015/09/22/cuba-religion-pope-francis-visit/32551927/ . Religious history complicated in communist Cuba Alex Gomex article in USA today.

[217] The U.S. State Department estimates up to 10,000 such "house churches" exist.

With an all-encompassing brush, Fidel even shuttered the Jesuit high school that he and Raul attended.

Although his aim was to get rid of every trace of religion in Cuba, albeit at times with extreme methods, it was never accomplished.[218] After the 1989 collapse of the Berlin wall and the ensuing fall of this socialist regime, Castro modified his policy from open persecution to a form of tolerance. Most significant was the 1992 constitutional reform, which stated that the "Cuban State would shift from atheism to a secular state."[219] According to the constitution, "the state recognizes, respects, and guarantees freedom of religion." It also states that "different beliefs and religions enjoy the same considerations under the law." Furthermore, the legislation prohibits discrimination based on religion. It also declares the country a secular state, provides for the separation of church and state, and declares "the Communist Party of Cuba ...is the superior leading force of the society and the State..."[220]

According to an interview with Christian Solidarity Worldwide ("CSW") of Mario Barroso, "Castro's policy went from trying to destroy religion to manipulating it

---

[218] The Castro regime is widely recognized to have used executions, concentration camps, prison sentences to quash and oppress religion and other counter socialist movement.
[219] https://forbinfull.org/2016/12/02/life-in-cuba-under-the-castros/
[220] https://www.state.gov/j/drl/irf/

and religious groups."²²¹ The clearest expression of this is the Office of Religious Affairs ("ORA") of the Cuban communist party, an entity with great power dedicated to deciding what to allow and what to abolish [regarding religion], in line with the political interests of the Castro's.

The IRF reports the Cuban government continues to control most aspects of religious life with claims of harassing some religious leaders and their followers, by threats, detentions, confiscation of religious materials, and restrictions on travel. The IRF found that several religious leaders alleged attempted government expropriation of their property under the guise of under new zoning laws. In contrast to Pastor Barroso's experience, the 2015 IRF reported a continued increase in the ability of their members to conduct some charitable and educational projects, such as operating before- and after-school and community service programs and maintaining small libraries of religious materials, including fewer restrictions on the importation of bibles.²²²

In opposition to permitting bible-importation and

---

[221] Mario Felix Lleonart Barroso is a prominent Cuban Baptist pastor and human rights activist from Cuba. In the following interview with CSW, he shares his perspective as a Cuban national, on the recent death of Fidel Castro and the potential impact this could have on freedom of religion or belief (FoRB) on the island.
[222] https://www.state.gov/j/drl/irf/

community service programs, is the fact that religious groups are required to apply to the Ministry of Justice ("MOJ") for official recognition. The application process requires the group's location, their proposed leadership, and their funding source. If the MOJ decides that the group is duplicating the activities of another recognized group, it will deny recognition. Notwithstanding these hurdles, Cuba maintains religious demographic diversity with 60-70% Catholic and a host collection of others.[223] After visiting Cuba, this book's author found the most dynamic religious sect is Santeria. Many Afro-Cuban descendants practice this religion with roots in West Africa and the Congo River Basin. The former slaves commonly intermingled their native spiritual rituals cloaked under Catholicism, and some require Catholic baptism for full initiation.

In conclusion, consider the impacts of church in support of the Cuban people. Incrementally, religion continues

---

[223] The Roman Catholic Church estimates 60 to 70 percent of the population identify as Catholic. Membership in Protestant churches is estimated at 5 percent of the population. Pentecostals and Baptists are likely the largest Protestant denominations; the Assemblies of God reports approximately 110,000 members; and the four Baptist conventions estimate their combined membership at more than 100,000 members. Jehovah's Witnesses report approximately 96,000 members; Methodists estimate 36,000; Seventh-day Adventists, 35,000; Anglicans, 22,500; Presbyterians, 15,500; Quakers, 300; and The Church of Jesus Christ of Latter-day Saints (Mormons), 50. The Jewish community estimates it has 1,500 members, of whom 1,200 reside in Havana. According to the Islamic League, there are 2,000 to 3,000 Muslims residing in the country, of which an estimated 1,500 are Cubans. Other religious groups include Greek Orthodox, Russian Orthodox, Buddhists, and Bahais.

to make a comeback, since the government eased restrictions on open displays of religion. The regime allowed churches to reopen and in 2014 approved construction of the first new Catholic Church since the revolution in Sandino. Cuba has received two Popes John Paul II and most recent the Argentine-born Pope Francis. In fact, the Vatican was instrumental in the cutting the shackles of the adversarial past with Cuba's northern neighbor.

In December 2014, Cuban President Raul Castro thanked Pope Francis for his role in the secret talks that led to a prisoner swap between Cuba and the United States and the start of "a respectful dialogue" to restore full diplomatic relations.[224] The papal intervention went further to "break the logjam and change the course of U.S. policy towards Cuba" as one of the host cities for the nine secret meetings between the Cuba and U.S. negotiators. Moreover, when the talks were stalled, Benjamin Rhodes[225] and Robert Zuniga,[226] who represented the U.S., requested that the Vatican "move the ball forward." Using political savvy and influence, the U.S. delegates leveraged three U.S. Cardinals to urge the Holy Father to bring up the Cuba discussion with POTUS

---

[224] LeoGrande, William M., and Peter Kornbluh. Back Channel to Cuba: The Hidden History of Negotiations between Washington and Havana. Chapel Hill: The U of North Carolina Press, 2015. Print.
[225] Deputy National Security Advisor
[226] National Security Council senior director for Western Hemisphere Affairs

Obama's official visit.[227] After an hour-long conversation in the Pope's personal library, the Pontiff offered "his good offices" to broker and facilitate an accord.[228]

2.4 A Rainbow Coalition

Gay rights throughout the world have advanced at a snail's pace similar to an ant digesting an elephant. The U.S., Cuba, and Latin America are no different. All three have implemented gradual changes at the behest of a relentless national and international LGBTI mobilization combined with a global shift in perspective that gay rights are simply human rights. This section examines the role of courts in moving that agenda forward and illuminates the legal and political strategies used to confront that expansion in others.

2.41 LGBTI Development in Latin America

According to the casebook, Latin America is a region known for its profoundly entrenched homophobia, machismo, and patriarchy, and for the wholesale marginalization of lesbian, gay, bisexual, transsexual,

---

[227] LeoGrande, William M., and Peter Kornbluh. Back Channel to Cuba: The Hidden History of Negotiations between Washington and Havana. Chapel Hill: The U of North Carolina Press, 2015. Print. p. 444.
[228] LeoGrande, William M., and Peter Kornbluh. Back Channel to Cuba: The Hidden History of Negotiations between Washington and Havana. Chapel Hill: The U of North Carolina Press, 2015. Print. p. 444

and intersex (LGBTI) people.[229] Despite the historical opposition, LGBTI rights have made major advances leading to the surprising fact that the region now contains one-quarter of the world's countries where same-sex marriage has been legalized.[230] The progress varies across the region, "ranging from criminalization of homosexual acts in some countries to full legal equality, including same-sex marriage and adoption, in others."[231]

By way of example, the crux of the Costa Rican LGBTI rights litigation have pivoted on the questions of discrimination and equal treatment of LGBTI people. One specific example of litigation progress was the successful amparo filed for conjugal visits for gay prisoners in the Costa Rican Fourth Chamber Court. This court's acceptance of jurisprudence on issues affecting LGBTI people reveals the willingness of the Chamber to protect the rights of one of the most marginalized vulnerable groups of people: prisoners who are gay.[232]

The court ruled the regulation as unconstitutional. Siding with the Procuradora General, Ana Lorena Brenes, the Chamber found "there are no objective and fair reasons to discriminate against gay prisoners, using only sexual

---

[229] Latin American Casebook.
[230] Latin American Casebook.
[231] Latin American Casebook.
[232] Latin American Casebook.

preference as the parameter. This court further recognized "a fundamental legal principle in the country's constitution is the respect for the dignity of every human being and, consequently, the absolute prohibition of any discrimination against that dignity."

2.42 U.S. LGBTI Rights

The measured development of LGBTI rights in the U.S. is similar. In the post-WWII McCarthyism, the government viewed homosexuality as overt acts of perversion, which lacked the emotional stability of "normal" persons and were susceptible to blackmail. The American Psychiatric Association went even further and defined homosexuality as a mental disorder in the Diagnostic and Statistical Manual (DSM).[233] In the '50s and '60s, gay Americans routinely faced an anti-gay legal system with police raids on gay bars. One infamous instance of such raids was on June 28, 1969 at Stonewall Inn in the Greenwich Village neighborhood of New York City.

The Stonewall raids served as a powder keg that erupted into a series of spontaneous and violent demonstrations by members of the LGBTI community. With the backdrop of the '60s social protest and anti-war

---

[233] "Homosexuality, the Mental Illness that Went Away." Behaviorism and Mental Health. N.p., n.d. Web. 26 Apr. 2017. http://behaviorismandmentalhealth.com/2011/10/08/homosexuality-the-mental-illness-that-went-away/. American Psychiatric Association listed homosexuality in the Diagnostic and Statistical Manual (DSM) as a mental disorder.

sentiments, the Stonewall riots are widely recognized to constitute the single most important event leading to the gay liberation movement and the modern fight for LGBTI rights. Initially, the organizing efforts were scattered and discombobulated because of challenge of crossing gender, racial, generational, and even orientation obstacles, but by June 1970, the first gay pride marches were held in New York, Los Angeles, San Francisco, and Chicago which led to strategically structured gay rights organizations formed across the U.S. and the world.

After decades of protest and incremental progress, the foundation supporting the walls of discriminations began to buckle. One of strongest wrecking balls against gay discrimination was the Supreme Court's ruling in United States v Windsor, which struck down the heart of the federal Defense of Marriage Act in 2013 ("DOMA").[234] The repudiation of DOMA ushered in a cascade of federal court rulings invalidated marriage bans in 20 more states. The last bastion of hope for the same-sex opposition came from the Sixth Circuit's ruling in November 2014 upholding bans in Ohio, Michigan, Kentucky, and Tennessee which persuaded the "Supremes" to settle the confusion among the circuits in

---

[234] "A Constitutional Right." The Economist. The Economist Newspaper, 26 June 2015. Web. 26 Apr. 2017. http://www.economist.com/blogs/democracyinamerica/2015/06/gay-marriage-america.

Obergefell v Hodges.[235]

Justice Anthony Kennedy authored the opinion noting,

> ***"[t]he centrality of marriage to the human condition makes it unsurprising that the institution has existed for millennia and across civilizations", referring to sources from Confucius to Cicero:***

Likening the privacy right of marriage to contraception, family relationships, procreation, and childrearing, Justice Kennedy opined they are among the most intimate that an individual can make and are protected by the Constitution.[236]

Turning some of the once stalwart fountainhead opposition arguments inside out, Justice Kennedy opined:

> Excluding same-sex couples from marriage thus conflicts with a central premise of the right to marry. Without the recognition, stability, and predictability marriage offers, their children suffer the stigma of knowing their families are somehow lesser. They also

---

[235] 576 U.S. ___ (2015) official citation not reported yet.
[236] "A Constitutional Right." The Economist. The Economist Newspaper, 26 June 2015. Web. 26 Apr. 2017. http://www.economist.com/blogs/democracyinamerica/2015/06/gay-marriage-america .

> suffer the significant material costs of being raised by unmarried parents, relegated through no fault of their own to a more difficult and uncertain family life. The marriage laws at issue here thus harm and humiliate the children of same-sex couples.

Despite the monumental ruling by the high court, local state officials were left to enforce and uphold the new law. On September 3, 2015, in Morehead, Kentucky, the Rowan County Clerk Kim Davis was thrown in jail on a contempt of court charge for refusing to issue marriage licenses to same-sex couples. She claims the Supreme Court ruling conflicts with her Christian faith. She was ultimately released after the court was reassured that her deputies would properly process the marriage certificates.[237]

While the U.S. gay rights movement was slow as the "ant-eating elephant," administrative agencies have been quick to export U.S. newfound perspectives. In an effort to defend human rights and promote the inclusion of marginalized groups, the U.S. Agency for International Development ("U.S.A.I.D.") advances its support for the LGBTI community by an envoy:

---

[237] *Id.*

> **Advance long-term strategies to promote the rights of lesbian, gay, bisexual, transgender, and intersex persons**. On February 27, 2015, the Department appointed its first-ever Special Envoy for the Human Rights of LGBT Persons. The Department and USAID, which named its first LGBT Coordinator in March 2014, will expand and implement long-term strategies to address the homophobia that underlies discrimination against LGBTI persons. The Department will continue to manage the Global Equality Fund, an initiative supported by public and private donors that helps civil society advance human rights norms and provides emergency and preventive assistance to LGBTI activists. USAID will continue to engage in LGBTI programming through several channels, including the Human Rights Grants Program.

2.43 Cuba's Progress

In many ways, Cuba's gay rights progression is like the U.S. and the Latin American region; saving the legalization of same-sex marriage by the Castro-led government. Historically, the pre-revolutionary Cuba mirrored its hemispheric neighbors in criminalizing homosexuality and outcasting gays from mainstream society. Many gay men were in favor of the Revolution and even supported Fidel and his band of bearded brethren; however, despite professed egalitarianism, the LGBTI community found no more sympathy to the cause than by prior Cuban administrations. The revered Che Guevara contributed to the bigoted machismo with his definition of the socialist "New Man" in part necessitated a strong and unambiguously heterosexual male.[238]

Like his predecessors, Castro continued to uphold the Public Ostentation Law.[239] From 1965 to 1968, openly homosexual men were rounded up and incarcerated in UMAP (Military Units to Aid Production) camps designed to change them into the ideal heterosexual. Critics denounced the labor camps for their brutality. Additionally, in the Mariel Boat Lift of 1980, the Castro regime considered homosexual Cubans among other "undesirables" and expelled thousands of them. Further international criticism came from Cuba's quarantine (or incarceration) of HIV patients.

The late '80s attitudes shifted and accompanied the

---

[238] "From Persecution to Acceptance? The History of LGBT Rights in Cuba." The Council of Hemispheric Affairs. N.p., n.d. Web. 25 Apr. 2017. https://www.coha.org .
[239] The fundamental purpose of the law was to encourage the harassment of gay people who refused to stay in the closet.

elimination of legal penalties against gay men. Further progress came in 1988 when the National Commission on Sex Education observed that homophobia was intolerable and such bigotry should be countered by education. Then, the government repealed the 1938 Public Ostentation Law.

The '90s brought more progress. In 1993, at a sex education workshop Dr. Celestino Alverez explained that all laws regarding homosexuality had been repealed and that homophobia was a question of "prejudice, not persecution." In 1993, F*resas y Chocolate*[240] (Strawberries and Chocolate), a film critical of Cubans' LGBTI discrimination, was produced by the government-run Cuban film industry. Artists continued to advance progress in Cubans' attitudes to homosexuality as documented in the 1995 film, "Gay Cuba." The film combines interviews with gay men and lesbians, government officials and average citizens, with musical performances and gay pride parades. The interviews created a celebration of different sexualities and allowed gay Cubans to lead much more open lives.

After turning the reigns over to Raul, Fidel

---

[240] Jordan, David. "In Cuba, a Government Backed LGBT Rights Movement Battles Against a Culture of Machismo." Social Justice News Nexus. N.p., 10 Mar. 2017. Web. 26 Apr. 2017. http://www.sjnnchicago.medill.northwestern.edu%2fblog%2fcategory%2fcuba%2f&p=DevEx,5073.1.

acknowledged the mistreatment of gay men. Cuba's public support for gay rights changed when the *"Commandante en Jefe"* admitted in 2010, two years after stepping down from the presidency, that he had been wrong to discriminate against homosexuals, which he referred to as "a great injustice."[241]

President Raul Castro publicly declared his support for gay rights. Illustrated by progressive reforms under his administration, the government authorized doctors to perform sex change operations starting in June 2008. Further cementing this human rights policy swing is the strong backing of Raul's daughter Mariela Castro, who is also the director of CENESEX. The most audacious change came in 2011 when the Cuban parliament proposed a law permitting same-sex unions.

While the legislation failed, Cuba seems poised for more progress. The Cuban constitution currently defines marriage as the union between a man and a woman. CENESEX officials expect that gay marriage will be up for consideration at the 8th Congress of the Communist Party of Cuba in 2021, although Mariel Castro has advocated a shorter timeline for the change.[242]

---

[241] Trotta, Daniel. "Cubans celebrate gay rights, but marriage remains distant." Reuters. Thomson Reuters, 10 May 2014. Web. 26 Apr. 2017. http://www.reuters.com/article/us-cuba-gay-idUSKBN0DQ0J720140510.
[242] Trotta, Daniel.

Chapter 3: DEFINING CORPORATE COMPLIANCE WITH A REKINDLED U.S. & CUBA RELATIONSHIP

In the climate of warming diplomacy, American businesses considering entering the Cuban market must analyze and evaluate the diplomatic impact on their bottom line *vis-à-vis* corporate compliance. The research investigates whether Cuba is a viable option or whether the compliance constraints; regulatory framework; economic truths, and legal and political regime present an uncertain economic outcome.

3.1 Executive Summary

American companies can compete and make significant gains in Cuba by developing a comprehensive compliance program that accounts for the voluminous regulatory restrictions and socio-economic factors despite an uncertain political environment.

3.2 Thesis:

This chapter questions the concept of the warming of diplomatic relations and evaluates its impact on American businesses considering entering the Cuban market. The research investigates whether Cuba is a viable option or whether the compliance constraints; regulatory framework; economic truths, and legal and political regime present an uncertain economic outcome. To answer this question, this chapter 1) assesses whether Cuban and American citizens desire engagement policies; 2) explores advantages of entering the Cuban market by evaluating regulatory requirements and the legal, political, societal risks and challenges; and 3) examines the need for a comprehensive and robust compliance program to combat those risks.

The second portion of this research focuses on the lessons learned from other foreign companies operating in Cuba. After that, the considerations move to proof of principles of American businesses operating in Cuba. Lastly, the book ponders whether Cuba has the capacity to absorb demand of its northern neighbor's behemoth economic. In conclusion, the section predicts and estimates the two nations' path forward in the immediate future.

3.3 Background.

U.S.-Cuba relationship has been plagued by distrust and antagonism since 1959, the year Fidel Castro overthrew a U.S.-backed regime in Havana and established a socialist state allied with the Soviet Union. Likewise, many are aware that the successive U.S. administrations pursued policies intended to isolate the island country economically and diplomatically; sanctions which lasted longer than any other country. But most are likely unfamiliar with the many failed attempts to negotiate with the Castro regime by virtually each POTUS since freezing diplomatic relations. The Cuban government estimated in 2013 that more than fifty years of U.S. comprehensive embargo cost the economy more than $1 trillion.

Since U.S. Senator Barack Obama claimed the United States needed to "pursue direct diplomacy" with Cuba, experts like Claire Felter, Latin America expert at the Council on Foreign Relations, have pontificated what that direct pursuit would look like.[243] Ms. Felter and her colleagues recommend four key points: 1) reform and rapprochement; 2) lifting the embargo; 3) gaging public support; and 4) reacting to the Trump factor.[244] First, notwithstanding Obama's easing of some travel and trade restrictions, reform and rapprochement comes when the two nations exhibit mutual respect for the sovereignty of the other.[245]

Secondly, analysts agree the embargo must be lifted, but rarely do any of the stakeholders agree on how this will be done. The Washington divergence on what the United States should do to further encourage the warming trend, particularly on the question of the trade embargo, is the last major diplomatic obstacle on the road to normal relations.[246] Most Democrats, along with some Republicans, support ending the embargo immediately, which they hope spurs further liberalization and human rights improvements in Cuba. Alternatively, many Republican lawmakers insist the communist government needs to move first and institute greater reforms before the U.S. makes any

---

[243] Felter, Claire, Brianna Lee, James McBride, and Danielle Renwick. "U.S.-Cuba Relations." Council on Foreign Relations. Council on Foreign Relations, 03 Feb. 2017. Web. 29 Apr. 2017. http://www.cfr.org/cuba/us-cuba-relations/p11113.
[244] Id.
[245] Id.
[246] Id.

more concessions.[247]

Americans, Cubans, Hemispheric and global partners alike support full normalization. Illustrating these sentiments, a Pew Research poll conducted in early 2015 found 63 percent of Americans approved Obama's decision to resume diplomatic relations, while another poll found that 97 percent of Cubans thought normalization is a positive thing for the island.[248]

In 2016, a CBS News and the New York Times poll found that 55 percent of Americans favored ending the trade embargo with Cuba. Internationally, the support for normalization is overwhelming, especially in Latin America.[249] In 2016, the UN General Assembly approved a resolution condemning the U.S. embargo for the twenty-fifth consecutive year, with 191 member countries backing the resolution.[250] Hopefully, this consensus in public opinion moves the legislative branch toward reversing the Cuba Democracy Act of 1992 and the Cuban Liberty and Democratic Solidarity Act of 1996.

Trump's Presidency ushers in new uncertainties. For instance, early in his presidential campaign, then candidate Trump expressed support for the détente, but

---

[247] *Id.*
[248] *Id.*
[249] *Id.*
[250] *Id.*

later stated he would reverse Obama's reforms if the Castro government fails to release political prisoners and grant Cuban citizens more political and religious liberties.[251] Felter reminds readers that Trump is a businessman, and if he decides to retract the détente, fellow U.S. business leaders would likely provide significant opposition. These U.S.-based companies have invested heavily in new ventures in Cuba since the warming of relations, including Google, Airbnb, and Starwood Hotels & Resorts.[252]

3.4 Regulatory Framework.

3.4A. Cuban Assets Control Regulations

The United States has maintained a comprehensive embargo on business with Cuba since February 1962. The Cuban Assets Control Regulations ("CACR") broadly prohibit trade and investment with Cuba by "any person subject to the jurisdiction of the United States," defined to include foreign companies that are owned or controlled by U.S. persons. In 1996, the Congress codified a more rigorous set of sanctions in the form of the Cuban Liberty and Democratic Solidarity (LIBERTAD) Act, popularly known as the "Helms-Burton Act."[253]

---

[251] *Id.*
[252] *Id.*
[253] Cuban Liberty and Democratic Solidarity (LIBERTAD) Act of 1996, Pub. L. No. 104-114, 110 Stat. 785 (1996) (codified at 22 U.S.C. §§ 6021-6091 (2000)).

The President is authorized to suspend suits under Title III for six-month intervals upon reporting to Congress that "the suspension is necessary to the national interests of the United States and will expedite a transition to democracy in Cuba."[254] This authority has consistently been exercised. Statement on Action on Title III of the Cuban Liberty and Democratic Solidarity (LIBERTAD) Act of 1996.

3.4A1. *Previous Presidential Administrations.*

The embargo regulations do not ban travel itself, but place restrictions on any financial transactions related to travel to Cuba, which effectively result in a travel ban. Accordingly, from 1963 until 1977, travel to Cuba was effectively banned under the Cuban Assets Control Regulations (CACR) issued by the Treasury Department's Office of Foreign Assets Control (OFAC) to implement the embargo.[255] The Kennedy- Castro communications nearly sent us to World War III. Castro reached out to the Johnson administration, but by the time the Cuba Task force completed a national policy paper on the way ahead with Cuba, a new President was elected. Secretary Kissinger attempted communications under the Nixon/ Ford administration but Cuba's statements

---

[254] 22 U.S.C. § 6085(b)-(c).
[255] Sullivan, Mark P. "Cuba: U.S. Restrictions on Travel and Remittances." Congressional Research Service. CSR Report, 07 Feb. 2017. Web. 1 May 2017. https://fas.org/sgp/crs/row/RL31139.pdf.

on Puerto Rican independence and interference in Angola "destroyed any opportunity for improvement of relations."[256]

In 1977, the Carter Administration made changes to the regulations that essentially lifted the travel ban.[257] Castro had high regards for Carter as "a man of honor" viewed him as someone who wanted to fix the problems between the two nations. Carter felt open trade, commerce, and travel was the best route to regime change in Cuba, but the Africa problem and the "Freedom Flotilla" constricted the relations.[258]

In 1982, the Reagan and George H. W. Bush administrations made other changes to the CACR that once again restricted travel to Cuba, but allowed for travel-related transactions by certain categories of travelers. After the Soviet collapse, Cuba's loyalty to USSR was repaid by economic catastrophe. Bush declared that he would "normalize relations only if Cuba abandoned socialism and adopted multiparty electoral democracy,"[259] essentially Castro capitulation.

Under the Clinton Administration, there were several

---

[256] Leo Grande, William M., and Peter Kornbluh. Back channel to Cuba: the hidden history of negotiations between Washington and Havana. Updated ed. Chapel Hill: The U of North Carolina Press, 2015. Print.
[257] Sullivan, "Cuba"
[258] Leo Grande, "Back Channel"
[259] *Id.*

changes to the Treasury Department regulations, with some at first tightening the restrictions, and others later loosening the restrictions.[260] A perceptive political scientist, he went further right than Bush on the campaign trail in Little Havana, saying that Bush missed an opportunity to put the hammer down on Castro.[261] He also introduced the "wet foot, dry foot" policy. Ultimately, Clinton signed the Helms-Burton into law after the Brothers to the Rescue fiasco.

Under the George W. Bush Administration, the travel regulations were tightened significantly, with additional restrictions on family visits, educational travel, and travel for those involved in amateur and semi-professional international sports federation competitions. In addition, the categories of fully hosted travel and people-to-people educational exchanges unrelated to academic coursework were eliminated as permissible travel to Cuba. Bush also cracked down on those traveling to Cuba illegally, further restricted religious travel by changing licensing guidelines for such travel, and suspended the licenses of several travel service providers in Florida for license violations.[262] In 2006, Fidel surrendered the mantle of leadership to Raul

---

[260] Sullivan, "Cuba"
[261] Leo Grande, "Back Channel"
[262] Sullivan, "Cuba"

due to complications after surgery.[263]

3.4A2. Obama Regulations

During the elections for Bush II's replacement, U.S. Senator Barack Obama initiated the rumbling of conciliation by encouraging the pursuit of direct dialogue. Under the Obama Administration, Congress acted in March 2009 (P.L. 111-8) to ease restrictions on travel by Cuban Americans to visit their family in Cuba and on travel related to the marketing and sale of agricultural and medical goods to Cuba. In April 2009, President Obama went even further by announcing that all restrictions on family travel and on remittances to family members in Cuba would be lifted, and on September 3, 2009, the Treasury Department issued regulations implementing these policy changes. In January 2011, President Obama took further action to ease restrictions on travel and remittances to Cuba by providing new general licenses for travel involving educational and religious activities and restoring a specific license authorizing travel for people-to-people exchanges. Obama created a general license for remittances to religious organizations, and expanded the eligible U.S. airports with Cuba service, but in most respects, the policies were like those undertaken by

---

[263] Leo Grande, "Back Channel"

Clinton in 1999.[264]

As part of President Obama's policy shift of engagement with Cuba, which was announced in December 2014, the Administration significantly eased travel restrictions and remittances. Among the significant travel-related measures, the Administration authorized travel by general license for all 12 categories of travel to Cuba set forth in the CACR; eliminated traveler per diem limits; authorized general license travel for professional media or artistic productions as part of the travel category for those involved in the export, import, or transmission of information or informational materials; and authorized people-to-people educational travel for individuals. The Administration lifted the value limits authorized for personal use import by U.S. travelers as accompanied luggage.[265]

Regarding remittances, the Administration initially increased the dollar limits for so-called nonfamily or donative remittances and the amount of remittances that authorized travelers could carry to Cuba. It then removed the dollar limits altogether and provided a general license for remittances for humanitarian projects, support to the Cuban people, and the development of private businesses. Supporters of

---

[264] Sullivan, "Cuba"
[265] Sullivan, "Cuba"

change in U.S. policy toward Cuba, including some members on Capitol Hill, had been calling for President Obama to ease travel restrictions by authorizing general licenses for all categories of permitted travel. The President's actions were part his discretionary licensing authority pursuant to the embargo itself.[266]

Lifting all the restrictions on travel, however, would require legislative action. This is because of the codification of the embargo in Section 102(h) of the Cuban Liberty and Democratic Solidarity (LIBERTAD) Act of 1996 (P.L. 104-114); that act conditions the lifting of the embargo, including the travel restrictions, on the fulfillment of certain democratic conditions in Cuba. Moreover, a provision in the Trade Sanctions Reform and Export Enhancement Act of 2000 (TSRA; §910(b) of P.L. 106-387, Title IX) prevents the Administration from licensing travel for tourist activities, and defines such activities as any activity not expressly authorized in the 12 broad categories of travel set forth in the CACR regulations.[267]

Pursuant to Obama's vision, OFAC issued four additional rounds of regulatory changes to the CACR in September 2015 and January, March, and October 2016 that further eased the travel restrictions. Among the changes are the

---

[266] *Id.*
[267] *Id.*

following:[268]

September 2015. OFAC amended the regulations to allow close relatives to visit or accompany authorized travelers to Cuba for additional activities. The changes also allowed all authorized travelers to open and maintain bank accounts in Cuba to access funds for authorized transactions. Transportation by vessel of authorized travelers between the United States and Cuba was also authorized by general license, and certain related lodging aboard vessels used for such travel was authorized (related to ferry and cruise ship travel). Simultaneously, the Commerce Department amended the Export Administration Regulations (EAR), issuing license exceptions authorizing temporary sojourns for cargo and passenger vessels to Cuba.

January 2016. OFAC amended the CACR to authorize travel-related transactions related to professional media or artistic productions of information or informational materials for exportation, importation, or transmission, which included the filming or production of media programs, the recording of music, and the creation of artworks in Cuba. Travel for humanitarian projects was also expanded to include disaster preparedness and response.

---

[268] *Id.*

March 2016. OFAC amended the CACR to allow individuals to travel to Cuba for individual people-to-people educational travel. According to the Treasury Department, the change is intended to make such travel to Cuba more accessible and less expensive for U.S. citizens and will increase opportunities for direct engagement between Cubans and Americans.

October 2016. OFAC amended the CACR, removing the value limit for Cuban products that U.S. travelers to Cuba (as well as U.S. travelers to third countries) can import into the United States as accompanied luggage for personal use.

3.4A3. Candidate Trump

In a Daily Caller interview, Citizen Trump opined, "I think its fine. But we should have made a better deal. The concept of opening with Cuba — 50 years is enough — the concept of opening with Cuba is fine. I think we should have made a stronger deal." Speaking at a South Florida rally -- in a state with a heavy Cuban voting bloc – he branded Obama's deal as uneven and benefiting "only the Castro regime."[269] Then after the campaign, President-elect Trump tweeted, "If Cuba is unwilling to make a better deal for the Cuban people, the

---

[269] Diamond, Jeremy. "Trump shifts on Cuba, says he would reverse Obama's deal." CNN. Cable News Network, 16 Sept. 2016. Web. 04 May 2017. http://www.cnn.com/2016/09/16/politics/donald-trump-cuba/index.html.

Cuban/American people and the U.S. as a whole, I will terminate deal."[270]

3.4A4. President Trump's First One Hundred Days and Beyond

Press Secretary Sean Spicer advised, "President Trump will take a full review of America's foreign policy towards Cuba." The President will look at "all" aspects of how the US deals with Cuba keying in on human rights.[271] Critics continue to surmise how the nations even get this far. Experts like author Jorge Dominguez opine that Cuba's communist regime has never allowed this much susceptibility to the outside world's influence.[272]

Dominguez and his collaborators analyzed the complexities of the bilateral dynamics. The collaborators correctly suggest that not only a milieu of issues is involved, but also the variation and rotation of key initiators. For instance, consider the multi-layers in the country, regional, and transnational aspects. Another focus to consider is the new players' rise to power and

---

[270] Damien Cave, Azam Ahmed, and Julie Hirschfeld Davis. "Donald Trump's Threat to Close Door Reopens Old Wounds in Cuba." The New York Times. The New York Times, 28 Nov. 2016. Web. 04 May 2017. https://www.nytimes.com/2016/11/28/us/politics/cuba-trump-obama.html.

[271] Batchelor, Tom. "Donald Trump 'reviewing Cuba policy', says White House." The Independent UK. N.p., 03 Feb. 2017. Web. 04 May 2017. http://www.independent.co.uk/news/world/americas/donald-trump-cuba-white-house-policy-review-a7562201.html.

[272] Dominguez, Jorge I., Rafael M. Hernandez, and Lorena G. Barberia. Debating U.S.-Cuban Relations How Should We Now Play Ball? 2nd Ed. New York: Routledge, 2017. Print.

their administrations.[273] With each putting their own spin on the bilateral cooperation between the two nations. With Obama already replaced by Trump and Raul replaced in early 2018 by the former first vice-president, Miguel Diaz-Canel, this presents unique forecasting challenges for attorneys and business analysts performing due diligence on Cuban compliance. Notwithstanding those challenges, the conclusion of this chapter will provide supported forecasting options.

3.4A5. Miguel's at the Helm

Miguel Diaz-Canel, the 17th President of Cuba, was born April 20, 1960 which makes him the island's first leader since Cuba's 1959 revolution to be born after it. Trained as an electronics engineer, President Diaz-Canel has often appeared more in tune with the times than his elderly revolutionary predecessors, Fidel and Raul, who ruled the Caribbean island for the past six decades. As a young provincial party chief, Diaz-Canel bucked party orthodoxy by backing an LGBT-friendly cultural center, donned a long- hair style and allegedly likes rock music.

Prior to assuming the Cuban Presidency, Diaz-Canel's political experience includes Minister of Higher Education and Deputy Prime Minister. Due to his age and savvy political nature, this author predicts that

---

[273] *Id.*

President Diaz-Canel will lead Cuba moderately before he succeeds Raul Castro as the First Secretary of the Communist Party of Cuba[274] scheduled to take place in 2021.

3.4B.   External Influences

3.4B1. Regional and Hemispheric Neighbors

While Cuba shows signs of susceptibility to outside political views regarding economic policy and human rights issues, the regional and hemispheric neighbors have closed ranks with the island. In June 2009 at the Organization of the American States, Secretary Clinton supported the Latin American states' move to repeal the 1962 suspension of Cuba's membership.[275]

3.4B2. United Nations' Concerns

The international community has essentially created an international customary law regarding the Helms-Burton law. On October 26, 2016, the annual somewhat, ritualistic U.N. General Assembly resolution, condemning the U.S. embargo, proposed every year since 1991, was employed by Cuba and many others to castigate the United States.[276] Both the U.S. and Israel,

---

[274] The de facto leader is the most powerful position in Cuba.
[275] Leo Grande, "Back Channel"
[276] Gladstone, Somini Sengupta and Rick. "U.S. Abstains in U.N. Vote Condemning Cuba Embargo." The New York Times. The New York Times, 26 Oct. 2016. Web. 04 May 2017.

abstained from the vote. The final tally for the resolution was 191 in favor, none opposed and the two abstentions.[277]

3.4B3. *Castro-out*

After the July 2006 changing of the guard, the world watched in anticipation of change. The experts see Raul as a pragmatist and that his approach would be different from Fidel. In fact, Raul even joked that Fidel leads one Cuba and he leads the other. Insinuating Fidel led the rigid communist hardliners, while he leads the more progressive Cuba.

3.4B4. *Castro-in*

With his more progressive posture, Raul Castro implemented corruption crackdowns and reveals his energy is set on projected Cuba's best days ahead. From his assumption of power and publicly communicating that he wanted open dialogue with the U.S., Raul has thrusted Cuba in a moral high ground. Likewise, the Cuban leader supported opening the Cuban economy to incorporate free market elements, including private enterprise and private ownership of homes and cars, for

---

https://www.nytimes.com/2016/10/27/world/americas/united-nations-cuba-embargo.html.
[277] *Id.*

the first time since the 1959 revolution that brought the communists to power.[278]

The scene is set. The die has been cast. The big question remains, "What Will Trump Do ("WWTD")?" While this question is always critical, foreign policy is especially important in a new administration. Will these other factors influence his decision? It is unclear now what action the Trump Administration might take regarding U.S. restrictions on travel and remittances. During the electoral campaign, then-candidate Trump said he would cancel or reverse President Obama's policy on Cuba unless Cuba acted to improve political freedom. After taking residence at 1600 Pennsylvania Avenue, the Administration maintains it is conducting a comprehensive review of U.S. policy toward Cuba.[279]

3.5. Cuba remains a viable option for foreign companies to sustain a profit despite the compliance restraints, regulatory framework, and socio-economic challenges.

3.5A. Cuban & American citizens support engagement policies.

Opinions are shifting. Cubans, Cuban Americans, and

---

[278] Bureau, Tracy Wilkinson Tribune Washington. "Kerry cancels trip to Cuba amid frictions over human rights." Miami Herald. N.p., 03 Mar. 2016. Web. 04 May 2017. http://www.miamiherald.com/news/nation-world/world/americas/cuba/article63942237.html.

[279] Sullivan, "Cuba"

Americans support engagement. In an op-ed posted on Huffington post, noted author and Professor of Government at American University, Washington D.C., William M. Leo Grande suggests due to the Obama administration's de-escalation and opening towards Cuba, opposition pundits spread "a variety of myths aimed at discrediting Obama's Cuba policy."[280] In keeping with the recent political debate climate and "alternative facts" scenery, Obama detractors hope to take full advantage and convince the new administration to overturn the diplomatic thawing with the southern neighbor. Professor Leo Grande lays out the "myths" point by counterpoint revealing mutual benefits shared by both nations:

For instance, some critics argue the people on the island don't get benefit from the American travel to Cuba. Likewise, this détente and human rights abandoned the anti-Castro protestors have worsened on the island since December 2014.

Similar critics argue that the American people specifically, the Cuban Americans are against engagement therefore supported a Trump hard line approach. Additionally, critics suggest the Americans

---

[280] Leo Grande, William M. "Eight Myths About Obama's Opening to Cuba." The Huffington Post. TheHuffingtonPost.com, 09 Jan. 2017. Web. 29 Apr. 2017. http://www.huffingtonpost.com/entry/eight-myths-about-obamas-opening-to-cuba_us_5873ad73e4b08052400ee471.

travel to Cuba has flattened and tapered off. This author disagrees.

3.5A1. Common Myths from the Cuban Perspective

Myth: The Cuban people do not benefit from tourism; all the money goes to the government.

Arguing the trickle-down effect, Leo Grande supposes in arguendo that even if all the revenue from tourism did go to the government—which it does not—the expansion of the tourist industry generates jobs and serves as a labor multiplier effect in local communities. He goes on to cite 2014 statistics that the tourist sector labor force is highly sought after by Cubans because it offers access to convertible currency tips that make it possible to have a decent standard of living. Some 755,600 Cubans worked in tourism representing 15.2% of the labor force—an increase of 16.9% since 2009 not considering the increase in U.S. visitors in the past two years.

Myth: Obama betrayed the Cuban people and Cuban dissidents to partner with the government.

Countering this myth, the professor cites an independent Washington Post poll revealing 97% of Cuban respondents thought better relations with the United States were "good for Cuba." Approximately half of these same respondents expressed unfavorable opinions of Raúl and Fidel Castro. So even among Cuban dissidents, there is support for Obama's policy because they see it as helping to create greater political space on the island and undercutting the government's excuse for limiting political liberties.[281]

Myth: Obama rescued the Cuban regime from economic and political collapse that was imminent because of the collapse of Venezuela.

Professor admits that the Venezuelan shock likely hurt, but economist estimates the loss of Venezuelan oil will cause a 2.9% fall in Cuba's GDP in 2017. According to Cuban born economist, Pavel Vidal, the nation's economy possesses more elasticity and not on the verge of collapse. Vidal reminds that the "GDP fell 35% during the 1990s when Cuba lost Soviet aid and the regime did not collapse.[282]

Myth: Cuba is strategically insignificant, so there's nothing to lose by taking a tough position demanding democracy.

This myth is laughable considering Cuba's strategic geographical location and proximity to the U.S. nearly triggered nuclear holocaust under the Kennedy administration. The two nations cooperate to combat

---

[281] Leo Grande, William M. "Eight Myths"
[282] *Id.*

narcotics trafficking and human smuggling and trafficking, which could be "crippled by a return to the policy of hostility" and likely alienating Latin America.[283] Additionally, China and Russia seeking to expand their influence not just in Cuba, illustrates the strategic nature of the country.

Myth: The Castro's are creating a family dynasty like North Korea.

Cuba has a constitutional succession process, and neither Fidel nor Raúl Castro's children are positioned to succeed them. Nothing supports Raul's son, Alejandro Castro, is in line to succeed his father a year from now, as some people speculate.[284] Raúl's daughter, Mariela Castro, heads the Cuban National Center for Sex Education and has been an outspoken advocate for LGBT rights and seems content for her public work to issues of sexuality. Raul's son-in-law, Colonel Luis Alberto Rodríguez, heads the economic branch of the armed forces which manages several major economic enterprises.[285] More importantly, Miguel Diaz-Canel, the first vice-president, no relation to the Castro's is tapped as the next leader of the nation if the Central Committee of the Cuban Communist Party, and the Political Bureau, where the key decisions are made, still want him in

---
[283] *Id.*
[284] *Id.*
[285] *Id.*

2018.

3.5A2. *Myths from an American Perspective*

Myth: The United States has gotten nothing in return for concessions made to Cuba.

Experts counter that the 2014 agreement resulted in the release of USAID subcontractor Alan Gross, CIA asset Rolando Sarraff Trujillo, and 53 political prisoners.[286] Additionally, the two neighbors have signed fifteen bilateral agreements on issues of mutual interest that benefit both countries, including environmental protection, health cooperation, counter-narcotics cooperation, and disaster prevention and response.[287] Professor Leo Grande contends restoring diplomatic relations allows U.S. diplomats to interact with the Cuban civil society and provide better counselor services to U.S. visitors and Cuban immigrants; however, if we break relations, the U.S. would have no diplomatic representation in Havana, whereas the Cubans will still have their UN mission in New York.[288]

Furthermore, he expounds that expanded trade benefits U.S. businesses and generates jobs, hence hundreds of companies conducting due diligence investigations for prospects there. These opportunities would shift to

---

[286] *Id.*
[287] *Id.*
[288] *Id.*

European and Asian competitors.[289] Moreover, he retorts Cuba's removal from the state-sponsored terrorism list "opened the door to cooperation on countering terrorism and transnational crime through the bilateral law enforcement dialogue" and 'enabled the United States and Cuba to cooperate to reach a peaceful settlement of the war in Colombia."[290] Finally, Leo Grande opines the "thawing" created U.S. regional benefits with allies across the western hemisphere, where the closed door policy hindered cooperation on key issues like "narcotics trafficking, migration, and trade."[291]

As recent as August 11, 2018, Cuba turned over suspected "ecoterrorist" Joseph Mahmoud Dibee. Tal Axelrod reported that the Department of Justice and the FBI alleges and ties Dibee to arson; conspiracy to commit arson; and conspiracy to destroy an energy facility in association with other domestic terrorist groups, i.e., Earth Liberation Front (ELF) and Animal Liberation Front (ALF). Mr. Dibee pleaded not guilty to various charges in Portland federal court.[292] This arrest and extradition illustrates Cuba's willingness to adhere to international

---

[289] *Id.*
[290] *Id.*
[291] *Id.*
[292] Axelrod, Tal. "Cuba Handed over U.S. Fugitive Described by the FBI as, "Domestic Terrorist" on Friday, According to NBC News." Apple News. N.p. 11 Aug. 2018. Web. 15 Aug. 2018.

norms and their effort to cooperate with the U.S. on some level albeit small.

3.5A2.a. Cuban Americans Attitudes Shifted.

Actual electoral numbers prove Cuban Americans did not vote overwhelmingly for Trump, whereas Hillary Clinton won South Florida by 100,000 more votes than Barack Obama did in 2012. Trump gained 52-54% of the Cuban American vote, only a few percentage points better than Mitt Romney and far below the 2-1 margins Republicans used to rack up before 2012.[293]

Part of this attitudinal shift comes by way of something as simple as Cuban Americans' desire to engage with their ancestral homeland. These Americans have heard countless stories from their grandparents' upbringing on the island. Likewise, these elders have revealed firsthand accounts of the devastating impact of the taking of their businesses and properties under the guise of the revolution. Many Cuban Americans are left between yearning to know about their "motherland" and their real and concrete feelings of animosity towards the government. Notwithstanding, these Americans are in many ways leading the exploratory return to Cuba.

Michelle Hernandez, a Californian yoga traveler, came to

---

[293] *Id.*

this realization in her life. In her 2016 article,[294] self-described "Cuban-American girl," Ms. Hernandez, writes she "grew up my ENTIRE life listening to daily stories about what it was like in Cuba and the provinces my maternal and paternal sides grew up in."[295] She refers to her great-grandparents' home-based *bodegita,* which was their family business. She speaks of the heartbreaking decision that her grandfather's family made when they departed Cuba when the *bodegita* was taken in 1965 under the Castro regime.

Ms. Hernandez has designs on visiting this ancestral home that still stands today. Furthermore, as a yoga traveler, she sees the island as a yoga retreat destination describing it as "magical." Her goal is "to educate those of Cuba's beautiful and one of a kind culture, through Yoga!" She is a perfect example of the generational shift and change many Cuban Americans experience and why the shift is trending toward more engagement.

3.5A2.b. Polls Don't Lie.

Florida International University's ("FIU") 2016 poll reflects a clear majority of Cuban Americans in support of engagement with an overwhelming 69% in support of the restoration of diplomatic relations and the 63%

---

[294] Hernandez, Michelle Your Cuba Travel. "Cuba Yoga Holiday Retreat" Apple News. N.p., 21 Jun. 2016. Web. 15 Aug 2018.
https://apple.news/AqRw5Dg2lS3O3VFyOSuh1OA
[295] *Id.*

opposed to continuing the economic embargo.

3.5A2.c. Travel Has Increased.

Various indicators drive pundits to speculate that the demand for Cuba may be flattening. Gregory Geronemus, co-CEO of smarTours, a tour company that's taken 3,000 Americans to Cuba, endorses the "softening in demand' concept. He attributes the slump in demand on the government nearly doubling the hotel prices on the island since 2105. Despite the government assurances of abatement efforts, the birth defects causing Zika virus serves as another driver of downward expectation.[296] This concern is countered by U.S. and Cuban doctors working together to fiercely combat the mosquito-borne virus.

A third source of skepticism is American Airlines cutting back flights to the island and switching to smaller planes on some routes.[297] An airline industry spokesman counters this concern with these are normal adjustments and global reservation experts detect no decrease in bookings for Cuba statistically 2015 to 2016 Jan-June comparison revealed an 80% increase in American visits.[298] The final argument is the uncertainty

---

[296] Harpaz, Beth J. "Is demand for travel to Cuba flattening?" AP News. Associated Press, 07 Dec. 2016. Web. 01 May 2017. https://apnews.com/a511af3afb46427eabc41181a7566a43.
[297] Harpaz, "Cuba flattening?"
[298] *Id.*

of President Trump factor, which is based largely on conflicting tweets. This speculation is unfounded simply because betting on what the Trump administration will or won't do is an effort in futility. Ultimately, the facts don't support the Cuba travel demand flattening idea. Look at the numbers, like the Weekly Chart: A Snapshot of U.S.- Cuba Travel and Trade Today.[299]

All tweets aside, President Trump is doing what any responsible leader should do with the keys to the stability and welfare of the world's largest economy, -- conducting a full review. Anyone suggesting anything else is irrational. What would shareholders expect from a new CEO leading a corporation? Look. Assess. Evaluate. Re-assess. Decide. The administration must make a deliberate and strategic decision based on many factors, the fountainhead of which is U.S. best interest.

"While the Trump administration reviews the U.S. policy towards Cuba, more Americans are traveling to the island and U.S. exports there have increased for the first time in three years.[300] According to Ms. Gonzales, 74% more Americans traveled to the island 2016. Additionally, Cuba is predicted to cross 4 million total

---

[299] Gonzalez, Elizabeth. "Weekly Chart: A Snapshot of U.S.-Cuba Travel and Trade Today." AS/COA. N.p., 07 Feb. 2017. Web. 01 May 2017. http://www.as-coa.org/articles/weekly-chart-snapshot-us-cuba-travel-and-trade-today.
[300] Gonzalez, "Weekly Snapshot"

visitors in 2017. See chart below.[301] From a business perspective, this is the sweet spot. At $25 per month, most Cubans won't be able to afford nonessential American products in the immediate terms; however, 4 million tourists that travel to Cuba and stay in the overpriced resorts can afford these products manufactured or exported from the U.S. How does American businesses leverage this clientele with disposable income?

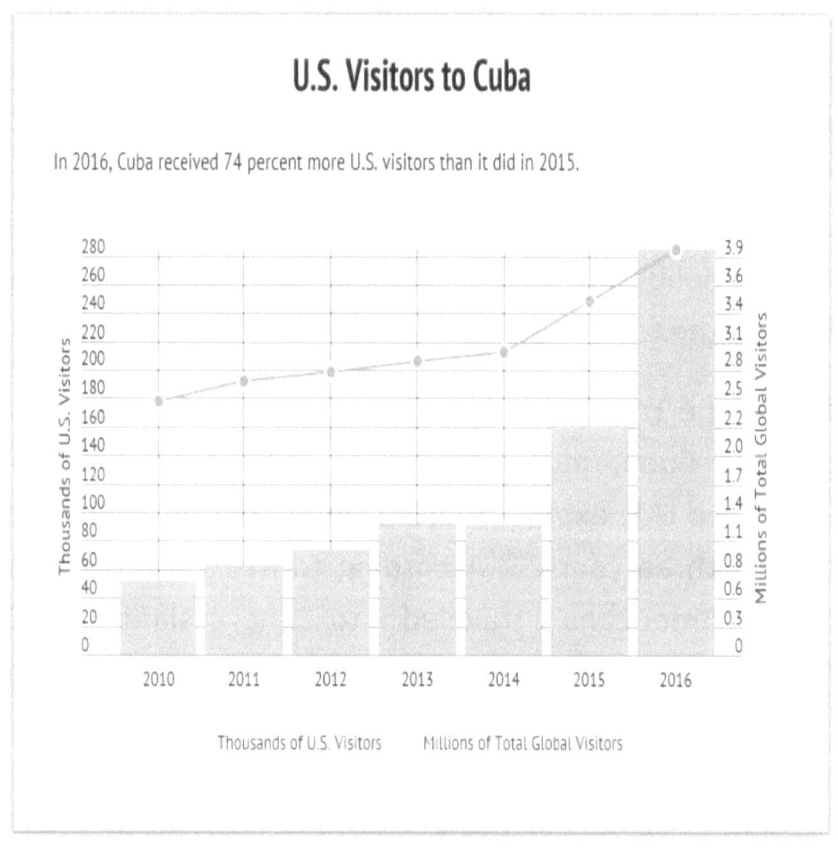

---

[301] *Id.*

3.5A2.d. The Trump Effect on Traveling to Cuba.

As President Trump's administration developed his Cuba policy initiatives, he directed Treasury and OFAC to make specific changes restricting or reeling-in some Americans' ability to travel to the neighboring island. Specifically, President Trump gave a speech in June 2017 alluding to the changes. In November 2017, the changes went into effect. Under the Trump changes, most "individual" visits to Cuba will no longer be allowed, and U.S. citizens will again have to travel as part of groups licensed by the Treasury Department for specific purposes, accompanied by a group representative.[302] This really just tightens up the Obama initiatives that gave rise to many Americans who were traveling for a wanderlust (leisure) experience, which is in direct violation of the Helms-Burton Act. Under Obama's opening, the "honor system" of individualized travel provided little to no auditable accountability.

Trumps changes also enforces the spirit and letter of the congressionally enacted embargo, which is designed to restrict Americans from contributing financial support to the communist regime. U.S. Senator Bob Menendez (D-N.J.) supports the policy re-tightening, opining that it is a

---

[302] DeYoung, Karen. "White House implements new Cuba policy restricting travel and trade" Washington Post, N.p. 08 Nov. 2017. Web. 15 August 2018. http://wapo.st/2Av7l2f?tid=ss_mail&utm_term=.eadd2007499e

step in the right direction.

An anonymous White House official briefed press members that the policies instruct Treasury and OFAC to steer economic activities away from the Cuban military, intelligence and security services... and encourage the government to move toward greater economic freedom" for the Cuban people.[303] According to Karen DeYoung, a Washington Post reporter, "These regulations bar Americans from staying at a long list of hotels and from patronizing restaurants, stores and other enterprises that the State Department has determined are owned by or benefit members of the Cuban government, specifically its security services."[304]

3.5A2.d. So What, Can You Travel to Cuba?

"Yes!" Eli Arroyo proudly exclaims in his Your Cuba Travel article.[305] Mr. Arroyo addresses the Trump policy shift as it relates to average Americans. He explains, "Yes, travel to Cuba is still allowed" under the Group people-to-people category. Travel is educational travel not involving academic study pursuant to a degree program that takes place under the auspices of an

---

[303] *Id.*
[304] Karen DeYoung is an associate editor and senior national security correspondent for The Post. In more than three decades at the paper, she has served as bureau chief in Latin America and in London and as correspondent covering the White House, U.S. foreign policy and the intelligence community.
[305] Arroyo, Eli. "YES! AMERICANS CAN STILL TRAVEL TO CUBA!!!" Your Cuba Travel, N.p. 18 Jun. 2017. Web. 15 Aug. 2018.

organization that is subject to U.S. jurisdiction that sponsors such exchanges to promote people-to-people contact. He correctly warns those utilizing this travel authorization must maintain a full-time schedule of educational exchange activities that are intended to enhance contact with the Cuban people, support civil society in Cuba, or promote the Cuban people's independence from Cuban authorities, and that will result in meaningful interaction between the traveler and individuals in Cuba.

This means don't fall into the trap of partying all night and then recovering all day and never engaging with the Cuban people. He goes on to remind travelers that an agent from your OFAC licensed traveling group must accompany each group to ensure that each traveler maintains a full-time schedule of educational exchange activities. Under Trump's OFAC amendments, travelers may be required to produce these schedules. Certain traveling groups exclusively use Air-BnB homes or other privately-owned homes, automobiles and restaurants in order to maximize travel benefits to the Cuban people, while strictly complying with the regulatory changes.

3.5B. *Advantages of the Cuban Market*

American businesses are naturally concerned about the protection of their investments and inquire what is being done to help them. How are American business interest protected without a bilateral investment treaty? What encourages the Cuban people to trust American businesses as brands and institutions? Is the government reaching out to the Cuban people? The United States is represented in Cuba by the U.S. Embassy in Havana.

The Office of Cuban Affairs and the U.S. Embassy in Havana formulates U.S. policy toward Cuba and provides an overview of Cuban political and economic conditions.[306] Together they advance U.S. policies toward Cuba focused on encouraging democratic and economic reforms; supporting the development of civil society in Cuba; promoting respect for human rights; and supporting the Cuban people. The U.S. continues to take steps to reach out to the Cuban people in support of their desire to freely determine their country's future.[307]

Businessmen further question the political leverage that the U.S. is deploying. Did all the secret meetings help pave a way to help business? Did the Obama trip do anything to excite the U.S. business interest? Did the trip do anything to invigorate the business community as potential investors in Cuba? What is the follow through?

---

[306] "U.S. Relations with Cuba." U.S. Department of State. U.S. Department of State: Bureau of Western Hemisphere Affairs, 07 Sept. 2016. Web. 29 Apr. 2017. https://www.state.gov/p/wha/ci/cu/.
[307] "U.S. Relations with Cuba."

How will the political détente increase confidence in investing in Cuba? President Obama's trip to Cuba in March 2016 marked a historic milestone in the normalization process between the United States and Cuba.[308]

Furthermore, the U.S. reaches out to the Cuban people by fostering increased people-to-people exchanges, encouraging the development of telecommunications and the internet, and creating opportunities for U.S. businesses to support the growth of Cuba's nascent private sector. The growing internet provides leverage to inform the people of the best business choices and objective reputation of the market leaders. Through the opening of embassies, the United States is now able to engage more broadly across all sectors of Cuban society, including the government, civil society, and the public.[309]

Agricultural and food service businesses conducting due diligence must focus on logistics and supply chain management. Although economic sanctions remain in place, the U.S. is one of Cuba's primary suppliers of food and agricultural products, with exports of those goods valued at $149 million in 2015. Additionally, Cuba receives significant humanitarian goods from the U.S., including medicines and medical products. Remittances

---

[308] *Id.*
[309] *Id.*

from the America, estimated $3 billion for 2015 play an important role in Cuba's state-controlled economy.[310]

Several reports illustrate the advantages of doing business on the island. Those advantages include U.S. banking easements; infrastructural development; and new license exceptions. Additionally, supporters tout the highly-educated workforce; proximity to the U.S.; and the diplomatic efforts taken by the U.S.

For instance, Baker-Botts reports new banking regulations permit "U-turn" transactions making it easier for businesses in Cuba to transact in American dollars. Additionally, U.S. banks may now process U.S. dollar monetary instruments presented by Cuban financial institutions through third-country banks. Nonetheless, challenges persist.[311]

Besides all the political support, businesses want to see capital investments. U.S. investors must investigate the Port of Mariel.[312] Cuba describes it as a strategic project for Cuban foreign trade. The Special Development Zone Mariel (ZEDM), is expected to be the main port of entry

---

[310] *Id.*
[311] Baker Botts, LLP. "Challenges of Doing Business in Iran and Cuba | Ideas | Ideas." N.p., 21 Apr. 2016. Web. 01 May 2017.
http://www.bakerbotts.com/ideas/publications/2016/04/pe-report-a-adams.
[312] HavanaJournal.com. "Port of Mariel information from Cuba Foreign Trade magazine." Havana Journal. N.p., 09 Feb. 2015. Web. 30 Apr. 2017.
http://havanajournal.com/business/entry/port-of-mariel-information-from-cuba-foreign-trade-magazine/.

and exit for Cuban foreign trade and a major development pole located in the center of trade in the Caribbean and the Americas.[313] The Cuban Council of Ministries responsible for its administration of envision Puerto Mariel as a special zone of world class, with high-level technology services and productions, a multi-modal logistics services provider, which provide support, protection and excellent services to the users and concessionaires, based on the renowned experience of the human capital, a modern, effective and efficient organizational performance and the privileged geographical position of the island.[314] Cuban Minister of Foreign Trade and Investment Rodrigo Malmierca Díaz avers the project as an economic engine for Cuba[315] and touts the Special Development Zone's ("ZED") legal framework.

Cuban officials further stress the streamlined approval process as a bureaucratic advantage. According to the 2016-2017 portfolio, there are only 2 levels: Director-General of the ZED Mariel Office and the Council of Ministers, for a maximum duration of 65 days from the presentation of the file. An efficient "One-Stop Shop" system frees investors from bureaucratic charges and processes all needed documents, permits, licenses and

---

[313] Havana Journal.
[314] *Id.*
[315] *Id.*

authorizations on their behalf.[316]

Revisions to licensing exceptions allow easier compliance.[317] In furtherance of Obama's policy to support the Cuban people, BIS amended the code of federal regulations 15 CFR 740 and 15 CFR 746. This amendment provided a license exception to allow cargo aboard aircraft to transit Cuba when that cargo is bound for destinations other than Cuba. This rule also authorizes export and re-export of certain items sold directly to individuals in Cuba under a license exception.[318] Finally, this rule revises the lists of ineligible Cuban officials for purposes of certain license exceptions. BIS implemented the previous administration's policy of increasing engagement and commerce that benefits the Cuban people.

To be eligible, the exports or re-exports must be sold directly to eligible individuals in Cuba for their personal use or their immediate family's personal use eligible for License Exception SCP. To be eligible, the items must be designated as EAR99 or controlled on the Commerce

---

[316] The Ministry of Foreign Commerce and Investment. "Cuba: Portfolio of Opportunities for Foreign Investment, 2016–17." Foreign Affairs. N.p., 13 Feb. 2017. Web. 30 Apr. 2017. https://www.foreignaffairs.com/reviews/capsule-review/2017-02-13/cuba-portfolio-opportunities-foreign-investment-2016-17.

[317] "Cuba: Revisions to License Exceptions." Federal Register. Bureau of Industry and Security, 17 Oct. 2016. Web. 30 Apr. 2017. https://www.federalregister.gov/documents/2016/10/17/2016-25034/cuba-revisions-to-license-exceptions.

[318] "Cuba: Revisions to License Exceptions."

Control List (CCL) (Supplement No. 1 to Part 774 of the EAR) only for anti-terrorism reasons.[319]

U.S. companies are starting to line up to conduct authorized business and due diligence in Cuba. In the agricultural industry, fruit companies are desirous candidates to enter the Cuban market. Sun-Maid Growers, the California dried fruit company where Chris Rosander heads international market development, currently gets its mangoes from Thailand. While on a fact-finding tour at a Cuban mango grove Rosander had a revelation: "Why don't we import mangoes from Cuba; 90 miles from the U.S. instead of halfway around the world" in Thailand.[320]

Some skeptics believe real trade will commence when Congress drops the embargo. Rosander readily admits his mango export dreams are not feasible under current U.S. regulations. Sun-Maid is a member of a U.S. agricultural lobbying group that urges Congress to end the trade embargo. In the meantime, plans to lay the groundwork; meet with Cuban mango farmers this year; and inquire whether they would have to change their growing process to meet U.S. sanitation standards.[321]

---

[319] *Id.*
[320] Linthicum, Kate. "U.S. Companies Line Up to Do Business in Cuba." Los Angeles Times. Los Angeles Times, 25 Mar.2016. Web. 29 Apr. 2017. http://www.latimes.com/world/mexico-americas/la-fg-cuba-gold-rush-20160325-story.html.
[321] *Id.*

Many consultants advise clients to develop comprehensive plan with a long-range strategy focusing on branding and building goodwill.[322]

3.5B.1. The Trump Effect on Cuban Business' Dreams

American business dreams are severely impacted under Trump's policy. Commercial relations with Cuba are restricted to prevent any exchanges with the 180 entities on the State Department's list. Trumps' changes would not affect certain existing transactions. For visitors, that means anyone who has "completed at least one travel-related transaction (such as purchasing a flight or reserving accommodations) prior to" publication of the new regulations in the Federal Register on Thursday.

For businesses, all those who have signed contracts before publication may proceed with them, officials said.

3.5C. Voluminous Regulatory Requirements, Restrictions, and Risks Presents Pitfalls and Potential.

Certain advantages result from the predictability investing in a Cuba's communist government. With the passing of Law No. 118 and its complementary norms, a favorable business climate has been set up in Cuba. Other advantages are added to tax incentives and these invite foreign investors to choose Cuba as investment

---

[322] *Id.*

territory.[323] Among these advantages:

- Formulation of sectorial policies for identifying investment opportunities with foreign capital that permits access to the Cuban market and its consumers.
- Geographical location in the center of an expanding market.
- Highly qualified workforce.
- International agreements signed by Cuba with the Latin American Integration Association (ALADI, by its acronyms in Spanish), the Caribbean Community (CARICOM, by its acronyms in Spanish), the Bolivarian Alliance for the Peoples of Our America (ALBA, by its acronyms in Spanish), the Common Market of the South (MERCOSUR, by its acronyms in Spanish), the European Union (EU), the World Trade Organization (WTO, by its acronyms in Spanish).
- Governmental policy that prioritizes research and technological innovation.
- Basic infrastructure throughout the country: communications networks; over 20 airports; ports admitting deep-draft vessels; over 95% of national territory

---

[323] The Ministry of Foreign Commerce and Investment. "Cuba: Portfolio of Opportunities for Foreign Investment, 2016–17." Foreign Affairs. N.p., 13 Feb. 2017. Web. 30 Apr. 2017. https://www.foreignaffairs.com/reviews/capsule-review/2017-02-13/cuba-portfolio-opportunities-foreign-investment-2016-17.

with electrical power; rail and highway communication.

After hiring local counsel from a "bufete" to explain these laws and ensure compliance. Some of the legal regime for Foreign Investment includes:

- Law No. 118/2014: "Law of Foreign Investment".
- Decree No. 325/2014: "Regulations of the Law of Foreign Investment" of the Council of Ministers
- Resolution No. 46/2014 and No. 47/2014 of the Banco Central de Cuba
- Resolution No. 128/2014 and No. 129/2014 of the Ministry of Foreign Commerce and Investment
- Resolution No. 16/2014 and No. 42/2014 of the Ministry of Labor and Social Security

On the global stage the Cuban market continues to emerge regarding Foreign Investment.[324] Cuba has signed agreements to prevent double taxing with Spain, Barbados, Italy, Russia, Portugal, Qatar, Lebanon, China, Vietnam, Austria, Ukraine and Venezuela and it has signed 63 agreements for Promotion and Reciprocal

---

[324] "Cuba: Portfolio of Opportunities for Foreign Investment, 2016–17."

Protection of Investments (BITs). Nineteen are signed but not in force while one is terminated.

Cuba defines foreign investment as enterprises with 100% foreign capital; foreign investors can build up on national territory as:

> a. Natural persons acting on their own behalf;
> b. Juridical persons constituting a Cuban affiliate of the foreign entity which they own; or
> c. Juridical persons setting up a branch of a foreign entity.

Cuba's overarching theme and foreign investment policy principles are impressive. The principles mirror policies like most nations seeking foreign direct investments. In a nut shell, Cuba wants to conceive of foreign investment as a source for the country's short, mid, and long-range economic development.[325] The island's proposal objectives to attract foreign investment are linked to access to state-of-the-art technologies; securing managerial methods; diversifying and broadening export markets; replacing imports; access to foreign financing; creating new job sources; and securing greater incomes

---

[325] *Id.*

based on production.[326]

The Cuban government does not view repatriates' investments as foreign. While Law 118 briefs well, the expansive foreign investment policy provides no protection for repatriates. For example, Cuban American businessman Saul Berenthal owned 100% Cleber, LLC, a U.S. company that wants to assemble farm tractors using Cuban labor for the benefit of the Cuban people in the Mariel Special Development Zone near Havana.[327] Like many dual citizen Cuban Americans, Mr. Berenthal dreamed of investing in Cuba. Mr. Berenthal, a retired 73-year old software engineer, and his partner, Horace Clemmons under the Open Source Manufacturing model. In 2012 President Obama praised their venture as "the first business with 100 percent U.S. capital authorized to invest in Cuba in more than half a century."[328]

With a lot of enthusiasm, the two investors conjectured the communist government would approve their project. But their full embrace of Berenthal's Cuban roots backfired. While at the Havana International Fair,

---

[326] *Id.*
[327] Torresngameztorres@elnuevoherald.com, Nora Gámez. "Cuban American lost his business bid after obtaining permanent residence in Cuba." Miami Herald. N.p., 09 Jan. 2012. Web. 28 Apr. 2017. http://www.miamiherald.com/news/nation-world/world/americas/cuba/article125450659.html.
[328] *Id.*

he was advised that his proposal was rejected because the project failed to meet the Mariel requirements on technology and worker safety.[329] Pundits argue that the downfall was due to his repatriation and achieving his permanent residency status in Cuba, which put the government in a problematic position: 1) accept the project, even though it would break its own ban on large investments by Cubans who live on the island, or 2) reject the proposal using an indirect argument. Officials chose the latter.

According the Justice Ministry's website, the Cuban government does not recognize dual citizenship and follows the principle of "effective nationality." This tale is just one example of the questions the island's government will have to face if it wants to attract investments from the Cuban diaspora. Citing a report produced by the National Organization of Cuban Law Firms on the foreign investment law Torres offers, "Cuban citizens residing in the country cannot participate as partners in a joint venture. This law is designed to favor 'foreign investors' or Cubans living outside the country."

As in Berenthal's case, like the estimated 13,000 Cuban Americans approved by the Cuban Embassy in Washington, D.C. for repatriation in their native land,

---

[329] *Id.*

they cannot invest their money in Cuban companies — even though the country's Foreign Investment Law leaves open the possibility that Cubans with other nationalities may invest in areas such as tourism or energy.[330]

Apart from the government owned enterprises, establishing larger companies are allowed only for foreigners. Referred to as *cuentapropistas* (self-employed), private sector workers are authorized and permitted only to work for themselves and cannot legally establish companies to expand their work beyond a small scale. Economist Carmelo Mesa Lago opines that these restrictions are especially counterproductive when the economy is shrinking.[331] Like many critics, Torres finds it "totally crazy" that Cuba needs infrastructure investments in all sectors and requests for foreign direct investment initiatives should include Cubans who have the capacity to invest.[332]

3.5C1. Disadvantages and Pitfalls

Despite this historic policy shift and the regulatory changes accompanying it, Cuba remains largely off limits for U.S. business for several reasons. First, the statutory embargo against Cuba remains in place. As a result, U.S.

---

[330] *Id.*
[331] *Id.*
[332] *Id.*

entities are still generally prohibited from engaging in business activities in or with Cuba. Furthermore, the relief provided by the "easing" is narrow and subject to complex limitations and procedural requirements. Additional legal and practical constraints mean that doing business on the island continues to present difficulties. The communist country's government officials are adamant that the easing of U.S. sanctions does not signal the privatization of the Cuban economy. As a result, the primary access point and partner into the market continues to be the Cuban government.[333]

Other obvious pitfalls of doing business in Cuba include the codified Helms-Burton Act.[334] For the vast majority of American companies, doing business with Cuba remains illegal because the economic embargo still stands. Latin American commerce experts Pablo Alonso and Alec Lee advise American business leaders considering investing in Cuba to understand the current status of its economy, as well as the key factors that will influence its future. While Obama's policy easing was important, they are unlikely to significantly change the face of the Cuban economy. For nearly two decades Cuba's economic sluggishness is based on the regime's

---

[333] "Baker Botts"
[334] Lee, Pablo González Alonso Alec. "The Potential and Pitfalls of Doing Business in Cuba." Harvard Business Review. N.p., 21 Mar. 2016. Web. 29 Apr. 2017. https://hbr.org/2016/03/the-potential-and-pitfalls-of-doing-business-in-cuba.

inability to generate higher productivity. This has been motivated by three factors:

- Lack of capital investment. Fixed capital investment in Cuba represents just 10% of GDP, which is half the regional average, and this is not likely to change until the embargo is lifted facilitating the arrival of significant new foreign capital.[335]

- Stalled state economy.[336] The large and inefficient public sector severely constrains the country's ability to expand output. Without a true price mechanism to manage resource allocation, many state-run enterprises are insolvent and require implicit subsidies to stay afloat. Closing 24 state-owned enterprises for failing to meet productivity targets, the Cuban government has gradually shifted workers into the private sector, but still only 25% of the Cuban workforce is currently privately employed.

- Currency confusion. Cuba has a muddled dual currency system with two currencies,

---
[335] "Potential and Pitfalls"
[336] *Id.*

the convertible Peso (CUC) valued on par with the dollar (Warning exchange rate fees as high as 13%) and fully tradeable, and the Cuban Peso (CUP) valued at a rate of 24:1 with the dollar, which creates severe constraints for the development of Cuba's export sector. While calculations would suggest the convertible peso is over-valued, Cuban firms will need to see considerable devaluation to gain greater competitiveness.[337]

When it comes to market size, the island's government further exaggerates by using methodological inconsistencies. The Cuban government enacted a series of methodological changes that produced a jump in GDP of approximately 15%.[338]

Will the Communist Nation open itself to U.S. trade?[339] Cuba is a market of 11.2 million people just 90 miles from Florida, and it is in dire need of all types of products and services. But any progress in trade and investment depends largely on politics on both sides of

---

[337] *Id.*
[338] *Id.*
[339] Hoag, Christina. "Doing Business in Cuba: Will the communist nation open itself to U.S. trade?" SAGE Business Researcher. N.p., 11 Apr. 2016. Web. 30 Apr. 2017. http://businessresearcher.sagepub.com/sbr-1775-99546-2726283/20160411/doing-business-in-cuba.

the Florida Straits. As businesses and others ponder the possibilities, these are some of the questions they are asking: 1) Is Cuba ready for increased trade with the United States? 2) Is foreign investment safe in Cuba? 3) Can U.S. companies make money in Cuba?[340]

Some 50 American companies and entrepreneurs attended Cuba's 33rd Annual Havana International Fair in November 2015 ranging from multinational giants PepsiCo, Cargill, Caterpillar, Boeing, American Airlines, and Cuban-Americans and other commercial representatives.[341] Analysts point to business challenges persisting irrespective of Congress lifting the embargo including people's weak purchasing power, dilapidated and outdated infrastructure, not to mention the spotty internet.[342]

D.C. based lobbying group Engage Cuba's President James Williams advocates lifting the ban explaining, "This is not a static situation, Cuba is moving forward. We're missing out every day."[343]

Experts argue that the Cuban and American governments have different economic goals, whereas the U.S. desires to stimulate more private enterprises,

---

[340] Hoag, "Doing Business in Cuba"
[341] Id.
[342] Id.
[343] Id.

the Cubans prefer business deals bolstering their state-owned companies. Under the embargo, this creates a seam between what the Cuban's want and what U.S. businesses can do.[344]

More challenges include restrictions on investments; obsolete and obstructive financial systems; human resources solutions; and investor and investment protection. First, one chief complaint is that foreign investments are often done in joint ventures with state-owned enterprises, although companies can operate independently with management contracts. Another major concern is foreign businesses can't sell directly to Cubans or invest in the entrepreneurial small businesses like "*paladares*" or small farms. The financial system of dual currency with convertible pesos ("CUCs"), which can't be exchanged outside of the island and 25 times the value of the of the local pesos ("CUPs"), presents major concerns and the government's promise to unify the currency has not quenched those fears. Foreign companies are also concerned about the government employment agencies dictating their work force and worker's salaries and only pays the employees a fraction of that amount.

According to Jaime Suchlicki, University of Miami's Director at the Institute for Cuban and Cuban-American

---

[344] *Id.*

Studies, "This is not a modern working force. It's a form of slavery." Even if the employees were paid enough to send remittances earned in Cuba back to the U.S., chronic lack of hard currency raises more worries. Another lingering challenge is the fear of government blocking international companies' bank accounts when it ran out of hard currency.

Most importantly, critics cite safety concerns regarding foreign investment and investors. After operating an $80 million annual export business for two decades, Canadian Cy Tokmakjian was arrested by Cuban authorities and had $100 million in inventory and supplies was seized. Tokmakjian was sentenced on bribery charges to 15 years in prison. The legal regime presents further problems. For instance, the 2014 foreign investment law requires disputes settled in Cuban courts, although international arbitration clauses can be inserted. Ultimately, experts critical of entering the Cuban market raise concerns that an impending U.S. business must carefully assess the associated risks. From a corporate compliance perspective, foreign business must use a Cuban employment agency to hire employees.

Compliance with the Foreign Corrupt Practices Act ("FCPA") is still a requirement in Cuba for personnel subject to U.S. jurisdiction.[345] The restoration of diplomatic relations between the U.S. and Cuba is sure to bring new opportunities for U.S. businesses seeking to gain a foothold.[346] Like all investments, there are associated risks, particularly those related to corrupt payments to government officials prohibited under the FCPA.[347] Because the state runs virtually all significant business enterprises, it raises the possibility that any payment of a bribe related to not only traditional government functions such as permitting, licensing, and government contracting but also business deals that in other places would be strictly between private parties will be a violation of the FCPA. Enforceable by both SEC and Justice Department, FCPA makes it illegal to pay an official of a foreign government, or any "instrumentality" thereof, to obtain a business benefit.[348]

State workers with low wages discover additional sources of income, which is essential to surviving. This creates an environment ripe for bureaucrats, business managers even at a high-level to accept and expect bribes to boost their income. Transparency International scores Cuba's corruption climate with a 46 just below

---

[345] Oleynik, Timothy Belevetz and Ronald, and Holland & Knight Law Firm. "A Warning on Doing Business in Cuba." CNBC. CNBC, 30 July 2015. Web. 01 May 2017. http://www.cnbc.com/2015/07/30/a-warning-on-doing-business-in-cuba-commentary.html.
[346] Oleynik, "A Warning on Doing Business in Cuba."
[347] *Id.*
[348] *Id.*

Ghana and just above Oman.[349] With a lower transparency level, a bribe paid to an official to obtain a commercial benefit may be less likely to be discovered and disclosed but is no less illegal, at least under U.S. law.

In response, Cuba is countering corruption. Since assuming control of the government in 2008, President Raul Castro has an eye toward liberalizing the Cuban economy and initiated public corruption crack-down with big results.[350]

In 2011, numerous executives at Etecsa, a state-run telecom company, were arrested on corruption charges and its president suspended. Later that year, 14 Cuban public officials and businessmen along with a Chilean executive, each one employees of either the state-owned Cubana de Aviacion airline or Sol Y Son, a joint venture tourism company co-owned by the Cuban government and Chilean investors, were convicted of bribery.[351] Even a vice-minister of the sugar ministry and joint ventures executives were sentenced to as many as 20 years in prison in a steering scheme.[352]

While some critics argue that charges are often brought

---

[349] *Id.*
[350] *Id.*
[351] *Id.*
[352] *Id.*

to eliminate competitors of a favored business, there is no question that the threat of criminal penalties — in Cuba and in the United States — exists for those who are not prudent.[353] To counter this hazard, companies must implement vigorous compliance and training programs that educate employees of the company's expectations, standards, and moral fabric. As the thawing continues, U.S. businesses prepare to leverage new and profitable opportunities; however, a company must manage those prospects by watching for and mitigating FCPA risk. Robust compliance, relentless training program and anti-corruption culture is the best way to keep the DOJ and the SEC from derailing efforts to establishing a foothold in Cuba.[354]

Holding a dubious distinction of one of the worst places to do business, American businesses must exercise caution when the foreign investment destination only ranks above two other nations.[355] The London-based Economist Intelligence Unit ranks Cuba among the world's worst business environments – No. 80 of 82 nations surveyed, and the EIU estimates it will get worst ranking Cuba above Iran and Angola.[356]

Experts caution other practical warnings. A Sun-Sentinel

---

[353] *Id.*
[354] *Id.*
[355] "Havana Journal."
[356] *Id.*

examines international companies in communist-run Cuba face nightmares such as tight government regulations, supply shortages, sky-high utility bills, unmotivated workers, and dismal customer service.[357]

Jay Brickman, vice president of government services for Jacksonville, Fla.-based Crowley Maritime Corp agrees, "you've basically got one customer: the Cuban government." Maritime Corp shipping service hauls authorized U.S. food exports from Florida's Port Everglades to Cuba.[358] Foreign investment analysts warn that foreign developments have been more tolerated than embraced by authorities. "It's seen as bitter medicine, like castor oil," said independent economist, Oscar Espinosa Chepe in Havana. "Some hardliners call it 'ideological contamination.'"

Cuba's concentrated focus presents additional risks. Even the once welcomed smaller European limited retail operations are now being turned away, as Cuba's government expands its own restaurant and store network. Miriam Martinez, a spokeswoman at the Cuban Chamber of Commerce explains Cuba strategic focus is centered on pizzeria and clothiers.[359] For instance, Benetton's Cuba sales have dropped sharply, partly because of rising costs and import difficulties. The

---

[357] Id.
[358] Id.
[359] Id.

Italian retailer operated as many as five shops in Cuba in the 1990s, has closed at least two permanently, said Tania Hernandez, a manager of the Old Havana shop now temporarily shut amid renovations.[360]

Other factors making it more challenging for international firms to operate in Cuba which include:[361]

- Employer pays government for workers, but the state pockets most of the money.
- Increasingly must import through state agencies.
- High degree of theft, low productivity, weak customer service.
- High utility and transportation costs.
- Concern over judicial issues, since the government is a partner and also judge.
- Repeated need to renew visas and work permits.

3.5C2. *Extreme Bipartisanship*

Based on the consistent low polling of Congress and lack of progress, a common viewpoint is "Washington is immersed in an acid bath of partisanship."[362] The effort

---

[360] *Id.*
[361] *Id.*
[362] CDA. "Cuba Central News Brief:" Center for Democracy in the Americas Home Page. N.p., 16 Feb. 2017. Web. 01 May 2017.

to preserve and build on the past administration's opening to Cuba is going to be an uphill battle. The smart money, as former Pentagon official Frank Mora, is on those who want engagement to fail. Mora even bets against the airline industry executives representing carriers with routes to Cuba who met with President Trump in the White House (at least the transcripts didn't reveal any public comments) in February 2017.

Certain critics counter Mora's pessimism. According to Cuba Central News Brief, "Extreme Bipartisanship"[363] is bastion of cheerfulness and hope from the two-party system. One grain of optimism that can bring legislators together and build coalitions across party lines is Cuba.[364] Leani García, writing for Americas Quarterly, calls Representatives Rick Crawford of Arkansas, Tom Emmer of Minnesota, and Mark Sanford of South Carolina "The GOP Congressmen Who Could Sell Trump on Cuba."[365] The list of proposed bills to upend the embargo is getting longer and acquiring more bipartisan supporters. Congress has even formed the House Cuba Working Group, an informal advocacy group on Capitol Hill whose members by rule are drawn from both political parties. In a recent study examining the threats

---

http://democracyinamericas.org/cuba-central-news-brief-extreme-bipartisanship/.
[363] CDA. "Cuba Central News Brief:"
[364] Id.
[365] Id.

of corrosive partisanship, distrust, and dysfunction in Congress, the Brookings Institution views caucuses like the Cuba Working Group as offering a promising way to rebuild bipartisanship.[366]

3.5C3. Personal Risks

Enforcement and civil penalties are serious. Under the Trading with the Enemy Act, U.S. Treasury may impose civil fines up to $65,000 per violation of the Cuban Assets Control Regulations. According to OFAC, typical individual penalties have been much lower. Penalties against companies are generally much larger.[367]

---

[366] *Id.*
[367] Since April 2003, enforcement actions for the Cuba travel regulations have included penalties against the following companies: Metso Minerals, Zim American Israeli Shipping Company, Playboy Enterprises, Omega World Travel, Mr. Travel, Havanatur & Travel Service, American Airlines, Cuba Paquetes, MRP Group Inc., Air Jamaica, Trek Tours (Rhode Island), Premiere Travel of Ohio, Hialeah Gardens Immigration Agency, Only Believe Ministries (Ohio), the Salvation Army (Texas Division), Beau Rivage Resorts Inc. (Mississippi), E & J Gallo Winery (California), the Four Oaks Foundation (New York), Pioneer Valley Travel (Massachusetts), the International Bicycle Fund (Washington State), Augsburg College (Minnesota), the U.S./Cuba Labor Exchange (Michigan), Coda International Tours Inc. (Florida), Travelocity.com (Texas), American Express Company (Mexico), Lakes Community Credit Union (Michigan), Sonida International (New York), Journey Corporation Travel Management (New York), RMO Inc. (Colorado), Tours International America (California), Aerovacations Inc. (California), Agoda Company (Thailand), Center for Cross Cultural Study Inc. (Massachusetts), Priceline.com (Connecticut), Magic USA Tours (Florida), Philips Electronics of North America Corporation (New York), First Incentive Travel (Florida), American Express Travel Related Services Company (New York), World Fuel Services Corporation (Florida), Weatherford International Ltd. and its subsidiaries and affiliates, CWT B.V. (Netherlands), Decolar.com Inc. (Argentina), American International Group, Inc. (New York), Red Bull North America Inc. (California), and Gil Tours Travel Inc. (Pennsylvania). Many other companies

3.5C4. The Carters En Cuba (Jay-Z and Beyoncé)

In 2013 Jay-Z and Beyoncé were involved in a highly-publicized inquiry when some Congressional members strongly criticized the singers for traveling to Cuba. The legislators' main concern rested with whether their trip was primarily for tourism, which would be contrary to U.S. law and regulations.

The Treasury Department stated that the two singers were participating in an authorized people-to-people exchange trip organized by a group licensed by OFAC to conduct such trips (pursuant to 31 C.F.R. 515.565(b)(2) of the Cuban Assets Control Regulations). (In August 2014, the Treasury Department's Office of the Inspector General issued a report concluding that no U.S. sanctions were violated and that OFAC's decision not to pursue a formal investigation was reasonable.)[368] See the Memo on the following page.

---

have received penalties for violating other aspects of the Cuba embargo regulations, including some that have been assessed multimillion dollar penalties.
[368] U.S. Department of the Treasury, Office of Inspector General, "Terrorist Financing/Money Laundering: Review of Travel to Cuba by Shawn Carter and Beyoncé Knowles-Carter," Memorandum Report OIG-CA-14-014, August 20, 2014.

Memorandum Report

OIG-CA-14-014

TERRORIST FINANCING/MONEY LAUNDERING: Review of Travel to Cuba by Shawn Carter and Beyoncé Knowles-Carter

August 20, 2014

Office of Inspector General

Department of the Treasury

DEPARTMENT OF THE TREASURY
WASHINGTON, D.C. 20220

August 20, 2014

OFFICE OF
INSPECTOR GENERAL

OIG-CA-14-014

MEMORANDUM FOR ADAM J. SZUBIN
　　　　　　　　　DIRECTOR
　　　　　　　　　OFFICE OF FOREIGN ASSETS CONTROL

FROM:　　　　　Sharon Torosian /s/
　　　　　　　　Director, Boston Office

SUBJECT:　　　Review of Travel to Cuba by Shawn Carter and Beyoncé
　　　　　　　　Knowles-Carter

This memorandum represents the results of our review of a trip to Cuba by the couple Shawn Carter (whose stage name is Jay-Z) and Beyoncé Knowles-Carter (Beyoncé) to determine whether the trip violated U.S. sanctions. Based on our review of available documentation and applicable regulations and guidance, we found no indication that U.S. sanctions were violated, and we concluded that the Office of Foreign Assets Control's (OFAC) decision not to pursue a formal investigation was reasonable.

We shared a draft of the memorandum with OFAC management. In a written response, included as attachment 1, OFAC stated that it agreed with our conclusion that OFAC was reasonable in its determination that there was no apparent violation of U.S. sanctions with respect to the trip. OFAC had no additional comments. A distribution list for this memorandum is provided as attachment 2.

Background

In April 2013, various media reported that Jay-Z and Beyoncé celebrated their 5th wedding anniversary in Cuba. The reports prompted members of Congress to ask the Department of the Treasury (Treasury) whether the trip violated the U.S. travel ban to Cuba for tourist activities. According to Treasury's response, the trip did not violate U.S. sanctions and was licensed under OFAC's people-to-people educational exchange program. Our objective was to determine (1) OFAC's guidelines for travel to Cuba under the people-to-people educational

Page 3

Jay-Z and Beyoncé's Cuba Travel Activities

In early April 2013, Jay-Z and Beyoncé visited Cuba under an OFAC license issued to a non-profit organization that has a mission to promote education in the fields of art, architecture, and the decorative arts. The media reported the couple was celebrating their 5th wedding anniversary. The reports included some of the activities they engaged in during the 4-day trip. Our review found these activities were consistent with the activities for which OFAC authorized the people-to-people license.

For example, one article reported the trip included a visit to a children's theater group and several clubs, where the couple heard live music and occasionally took to the dance floor. According to the article, they also toured Cuba's top art school, where they met with young artists, and ate at some of Havana's privately run restaurants, known as "paladares."[3] One of the city's leading architects led the couple on an architectural tour of the Old City of Havana, during which the article stated the couple was mobbed by Cuban spectators.

We reviewed the OFAC case file for the non-profit organization. The case file included a renewal application filed in May 2012. We determined that a proposed itinerary included with the renewal application was consistent with OFAC's *Comprehensive Guidelines for License Applications to Engage in Travel-Related Transactions Involving Cuba*. These guidelines state that each traveler must have a full-time schedule of educational exchange activities that will result in meaningful interaction between the travelers and individuals in Cuba. The activities listed in the renewal application included a welcome dinner at a paladar, a guided walking tour of various neighborhoods in the Old City of Havana with a Cuban architect guide, a presentation of art students' work and an art studio visit guided by a Cuban professor, a visit to a local children's theater group, and a rehearsal at a practice studio of a Cuban dance company. According to the non-profit organization's renewal application, all of these activities serve the U.S. foreign policy goal of helping the Cuban people by facilitating exchanges with them and supporting the development of independent activity and civil society. OFAC did not object to these activities and renewed the non-profit organization's license in October 2012; that license was in effect during the period of Jay-Z and Beyoncé's travel to Cuba.

---

[3] A paladar is a restaurant that has been allowed by the Cuban government to operate in a private home. By eating in private residences, instead of state-run restaurants, diners support the economic independence of these establishments.

3.5C5. Business Risks

Businesses, whether incorporated, reporting to stockholders or unincorporated, accountable to the bottom-line, must exercise deliberate that it doesn't conflict with this OFAC regulations. Consider the following examples of American Express, ING Bank, and Paribas, and before you think, your business has lawyers, a war chest, and willingness to pursue litigation all the way to the Supreme Court, see *Regan v. Wald*. Sometimes businesses are successful because leaders make calculated risk assessment. Hopefully, the following cases will discourage such "envelope-pushing."

In July 2013, American Express Travel Related Services Inc. (TRS) agreed to pay $5.2 million for violations of the travel regulations from December 2005 to November 2011, when it issued more than 14,000 tickets for travel between Cuba and countries other than the United States. OFAC maintained that TRS expressed "reckless disregard for the CACR" because of similar apparent violations in 1995 and 1996, the lack of oversight by its U.S. management of TRS's foreign offices, and the failure to implement effective mechanisms for detecting Cuba travel bookings until late 2010 after having informed OFAC in 1995 and 1996 that it would do so.[369]

---

[369] Sullivan, "Cuba."

Another example to consider is ING Bank, N.V. of the Netherlands, which reached a $619-million settlement with OFAC in June 2012 for violating U.S. sanction regimes against Cuba, Iran, Burma, Sudan, and Libya. The Cuban sanctions violations accounted for most the bank's settlement. See U.S. Department of the Treasury, Office of Foreign Assets Control, "Enforcement Information for June 12, 2012."[370]

In a massive example of paying the costs for violating these sanctions, in June 2014, the French bank BNP Paribas, SA (BNPP) agreed to plead guilty for violating U.S. sanctions against Sudan, Iran, and Cuba by processing financial transactions involving those countries through the U.S. financial system. The company agreed to pay $8.97 billion in penalties, a record U.S fine. See U.S. Department of Justice, "BNP Paribas Agrees to Plead Guilty and to Pay $8.9 Billion for Illegally Processing Financial Transactions for Countries Subject to U.S. Economic Sanctions," press release, June 30, 2014.[371]

The U.S. Supreme Court is squarely supportive of restrictions for national security reasons. In a 5-4 decision, *Regan v. Wald*, 468 U.S. 222 (1984), the court rejected a challenge to the ban on travel to Cuba and

---

[370] Sullivan, "Cuba."
[371] *Id.*

asserted the executive branch's right to impose travel restrictions for national security reasons. The restrictions on travel-related transactions with Cuba imposed by the 1982 amendment to Regulation 560 do not violate the freedom to travel protected by the Due Process Clause of the Fifth Amendment. Cf. Zemel v. Rusk, 381 U. S. 1. Given the traditional deference to executive judgment in the realm of foreign policy, there is an adequate basis under the Due Process Clause to sustain the President's decision to curtail, by restricting travel, the flow of hard currency to Cuba that could be used in support of Cuban adventurism.[372]

3.5D. Comprehensive Compliance Program

With the massive amount of regulations from Helms-Burton, OFAC, and Cuba, potential investors must establish a comprehensive compliance program that navigates these regulations and ensures conformity. Ventures, small and large alike, are under growing pressure to comply with Health, Safety, and Environment (HSE) regulations. Irrespective of the industry, to meet the growing business challenges of complying with Health, Safety & Environmental, the company must conduct a value-adding cost benefit analysis of an in-house legal department and develop an outside counsel law office who can subscribe to a

---

[372] *Id.*

company like Bureau Veritas to navigate regulations. A multi-layered legal environment provides an integrated approach to these issues to keep their compliance costs low, avoid potential litigation and even to protect their corporate image.

3.5D1. Compliance HSE Management

Generally, the main aim of HSE Management is to reduce a company's risk of litigation. This is achieved by making sure the company complies with relevant regulations and by helping reduce the number of accidents occurring in the workplace.

These key benefits facilitated by legal and compliance departments, with outside counsel is systems-driven processes which include constantly monitoring changes to the law and carries out detailed assessments to confirm compliance. The best examples of good practice are noted, and used as benchmarks for other sites that need improvement. Using local Cuban experts, this approach should include litigation support; compliance audits; HSE training; due diligence for mergers and acquisitions; and outsourcing. HSE compliance improves corporate image by demonstrating commitment to HSE issues. Like all compliance, leadership must effectively communicate and ordain this concept. Managers at all levels must show importance to the value that the program offers. Likewise, the compliance program must be operationally focus, cost efficient, fully integrated with training, and housed in part with human resources and legal.

Business entering the Cuban market must include a total quality management system. Beyond ISO 9001 Certification and OHSAS 18001 for OHSAS, some companies offer certification to a large range of management system standards that include:

- § ISO 14001, ISO 45001, SA8000
- § IATF 16949
- § AS 9100 & EN 9100
- § TL 9000
- § ISO 28000 & TAPA
- § ISO 22000
- § ISO 27001

3.5D2. Bayer Bears an Exemplary Compliance Program

Bayer, an international pharmaceutical company, provides a great compliance example. Regardless of the size of the company operating in Cuba, leaders must have core values as to its moral identity irrespective of what is status quo for a business. A strong example of corporate compliance policy is Bayer.[373] Bayer provides an executive down definition of its values, stating "We define compliance as legally and ethically impeccable conduct by all employees in their daily work, because the way they carry out their duties affects the company's reputation. Bayer does not tolerate any violation of applicable laws, relevant codes of conduct or internal regulations."[374]

Bayer provides its employees *10 compliance principles and explains their corporate effect and impact on consumers:*

1. We compete fairly in every market (no price fixing and no cartels).
2. We act with integrity in all our business dealings (intolerant culture of corruption and bribery).
3. We balance economic growth with ecological and social responsibility (HSE).
4. We observe trade controls that regulate our global business (follow sanctions and prevent technologies from ending in the hands of prohibited parties).

---

[373] AG, Bayer. "Bayer's Corporate Compliance Policy." Bayer's Corporate Compliance Policy. Bayer, n.d. Web. 01 May 2017. https://www.bayer.com/en/corporate-compliance-policy.aspx.
[374] "Bayer's Corporate Compliance Policy."

5. We safeguard equal opportunity in securities trading (prevent insider trading).
6. We keep accurate books and records (transparent, accurate, reliable financials).
7. We treat each other with fairness and respect (fair treatment and respectful relations).
8. We protect and respect intellectual property rights (protect its own IP and doesn't incorporate other's intellectual property into our own work without permission).
9. We act in Bayer's best interest (alert managers of perceived conflicts and use objective criteria such as price, quality, reliability, and ability to meet technical standards).
10. Bayer strictly adheres to the laws designed to protect and secure the privacy and confidentiality of information about individuals (proper handling of personal, health, financial, and similar info).

Bayer's approach provides its employees blueprint. With training, rewards program, and oversight, their program will perform well. Any business contemplating the Cuban market must develop a similar strategy.

3.6. Foreign and American businesses currently operating in Cuba are finding success.

3.6A. International Community

3.6A.1. Canadian Sherritt International

International companies have already invented the wheel, so why reinvent it? Supporters of foreign business in Cuba claim that many businesses report smooth dealings. Sherritt International's CEO, David Pathe exalts, "We've been in Cuba for over 20 years," and considers the island remarkably stable business environment. Then, proponents point to one of the largest foreign investors France's Accor, which operates numerous hotels under management contracts and was approved to build a luxurious Sofitel So La Habana to serve foreign tourists. Like many of these deals, the financial and operational details are private; however, Cuba experts laud these deals as success stories to navigating the nebulous intricacies of foreign businesses on the island.[375]

Critics perceive this success as more isolated arguing that more businesses have left Cuba than have stayed. There were 400 foreign companies operating on the

---

[375] Hoag, "Doing Business in Cuba."

island in 2000 and 190 in 2013. Pro-embargo analysts opine that this illustrates the difficulty in doing business in Cuba.[376] Director of the U.S.-Cuba Democracy Political Action Committee, Maurico Claver-Carone argues that there is one business client, i.e., the Cuban government.[377] Brookings Institute senior fellow in foreign policy interjects, "The more common experience is frustration."[378]

3.6A.2. China

From commercial vehicles like trucks and buses to approximately $500 million for a golf resort, China is deepening its business footprint in Cuba. This investment posture helps the fellow Communist-run state survive a calamity in Venezuela, the island nation's oil-benefactor and further protect it against a possible Trump administration's rollback of U.S. detente.[379]

Cuba-China business relations appear strong. China exports to Cuba reached a record $1.9 billion in 2015, nearly 60 percent above the annual average of the previous ten years. In 2016, the exports dipped to $1.8 billion as the flow of oil and cash slowed from Venezuela

---

[376] *Id.*
[377] *Id.*
[378] *Id.*
[379] Frank, Mark. "China Piles Into Cuba As Venezuela Fades and Trump Looms." The Cuban Economy – La Economía Cubana. N.p., 14 Feb. 2017. Web. 23 May 2017. https://thecubaneconomy.com/articles/2017/02/china-piles-into-cuba-as-venezuela-fades-and-trump-looms/.

due to economic and political fiasco in the South American country, illustrating perhaps the end of the failed state's petro-diplomacy.

Analysts speculate that the world's second largest economy's doubling down is designed to gain a competitive business advantage over U.S. competitors in Cuba's opening market. Marc Frank argues China's role "leave[s] the island less exposed to the chance U.S. President Donald Trump's [potential] clamp down on travel to Cuba and tighten trade restrictions loosened by his predecessor Barack Obama." Mr. Frank further speculates that a deterioration in U.S.-China relations under Trump presumably could lead Beijing to dig in deeper in Cuba. China's growing trade as Cuba's largest creditor is supported by "soft credit" terms for the goods purchased.[380]

According to Ted Piccone of the Brookings Institute, "Trump's threats to increase pressure on China…" may force the Asian economic juggernaut to expand its footprint 90 miles off the U.S. coast. Cubans love what the Chinese more prominent products demonstrated by the tens of thousands that flock to the hundreds of Huwaei supplied Wi-Fi hot spots.

"When the Trump administration increases pressure on

---

[380] *Id.*

China ... China may decide to double down on its expanding footprint in the United States' neighborhood," said Ted Piccone, a Latin America analyst at the Brookings Institution think tank.[381]

The fellow communists relish in their euphoria of economic partnerships. The Beijing foreign ministry went as far as describing the union as "good comrades, brothers, and partners," and further offered that the decision to deepen its relations in Cuba "were not influenced by U.S. policy. The ministry's spokesperson opined that this demonstrates all countries have consistent expectations about Cuba's vast development potential.[382]

Ultimately, the Obama easing reduced China's prior reluctance about investing in Cuba based on fear of losing opportunities in the U.S. The Cuban government boasts the two nations renewable energy cooperation including a joint venture with Haier. Additionally, Cuba opened a Haier computer assembly plant producing 120,000 units yearly. Further cementing the Chinese footing, the two have projects ranging from pharmaceuticals, vehicle production, a Santiago de Cuba container terminal, (partially funded by $120 million Chinese development loan; and a series of bioelectricity

---

[381] *Id.*
[382] *Id.*

plants attached to sugar mills to name a few.

3.6A.3. United Kingdom

The British are coming, or more appropriately, the British will be there when American businesses get there. Take it from the Britons, who have been doing business in Cuba for years. Cuba has one of the worlds few remaining centrally planned economies. The state controls 90 percent of the economy and employs around 85 percent of the total workforce. Since Cuba and U.S. began talking, international business leaders have more interest due to the reduction of risks doing business on the island.

The UK sees advantages and weaknesses of engaging in business in Cuba. As for strengths, the UK Department for International Trade ("DIT") encourages trade due to the widely spoken English language; geographical strategic position; highly educated and skilled workforce; low labor costs; low crime and pollution rates. Despite the increasing opportunities, DIT observes challenges in the Cuban market:

- very slow decision-making, with most important business decisions being referred to high level government;
- all sales in Cuba are public sales, controlled by heavy regulation;

- payment delays are common;
- standard practice for the Cuban state to expect to buy on credit terms of 1 to 2 years potentially increased market competition due to easing of US sanctions; and
- U.S. extraterritorial fines but the UK Protection of Trading Interests Act & EU Blocking statute provides UK businesses some protection.[383]

3.6B. Most Americans won't be able to do business immediately.

Most U.S. businesses cannot trade with Cuba because of the embargo, which is held in place by several pieces of legislation. The embargo's future will depend on the U.S. political climate. Both houses of Congress — currently controlled by the Republican opposition — would have to pass legislation undoing provisions of the previous acts to end it. The Obama administration could not garner the consensus needed to pass embargo lifting legislation during an election year.[384]

---

[383] "Doing business in Cuba: Cuba trade and export guide."- GOV.UK. 18.Feb 2016. Web. 30 Apr. 2017.
https://www.gov.uk/government/publications/exporting-to-cuba/doing-business-in-cuba-cuba-trade-and-export-guide.

[384] Analysts, Stratfor. "Most U.S. companies won't be able to do business in Cuba for years." Market Watch. N.p., 26 Mar. 2016. Web. 30 Apr. 2017.

Cuba's national economic regulations require adjusting as well before the island is ready to receive significant foreign investment from the United States. Uncertainties will likely remain until Havana takes steps to address them, the most immediate of which is the dual exchange rate in the country. Cuba has two currencies: the peso (valued at roughly 23 pesos to the dollar) and the convertible peso (roughly equal in value to the dollar).[385]

The use of convertible pesos across the economy has created significant distortions. For example, measuring state firms' exact assets is difficult if balance sheets are presented in convertible pesos. But adjustments to the exchange rate could drive up inflation, making imported food items, which the island depends on, more expensive.[386]

How the communist committee deal with investment requests in the near term will also determine much of Cuba's success in attracting investment. Under the current system, ministries and government councils technically approve investments. In practice, final approval largely rests with the country's military elite, particularly Raul Castro's son-in-law, Gen. Luis Rodriguez

---

http://www.marketwatch.com/story/most-us-companies-wont-be-able-to-do-business-in-cuba-for-years-2016-03-26.
[385] *Id.*
[386] *Id.*

as stipulated by the country's 2014 investment law. Such a system could potentially raise transparency concerns for investors.

Cuba's close ties with the floundering Venezuelan energy sector also presents concerns. Cuba is a net importer of energy and takes in around 90,000 of the 118,000 barrels it consumes per day from Venezuela. As Venezuela enters a period of increasing political and economic instability, it could suddenly decide over the next few years to cut off energy shipments to Cuba — a decision that would be devastating to Havana. It would leave Cuba in a financially untenable situation and with an energy shortage that would seriously curtail electricity generation. (Most of Cuba's electric sector runs on fossil fuels.)[387]

Specific sectors such as tourism, which last year brought the island about $2 billion in reported revenue, will still benefit from Cuba's opening regardless of whether Cuba implements any economic reforms.[388]

3.6C. *Proof of Principles*

3.6C.1. *Tech*

Mack Kolarich, Co-Founder and VP of Product of Startup Angels, wrote an article providing insight and daily

---

[387] *Id.*
[388] *Id.*

tidbits regarding strengths and weaknesses of Cuba's entrepreneurial environment. While nothing on the list is earth-shattering with enlightenment, the enumeration covers practical concerns for foreign investors and startups.

Surprisingly enough, Cuba has a technology scene that is exceedingly tech savvy and committed to connecting with other communities. Due to the highly-educated population in general, this country is a breeding ground for an educated capital (Cuba claims 100% literacy, but critics, on the other hand, assert its more like 99%). Havana even held its first ever Startup Weekend in November 2015.[389] Although Cuban software developers earn much more than the average Cuban's $20-$30 paycheck, the salary is still below $500 per month. Some startups monthly payroll is $5,000 USD.[390] While art has been a mainstay good income earner and best avenues for traveling abroad, this wealth of creative talent is likely to spill over into other parts of the Cuban economy foreshadows a future role in technology innovation.[391] Additionally, developer talent is abundant and IT outsourcing is likely the most affordable quick turnaround for an investment due to the country

---

[389] Kolarich, Mack. "17 Things You Need to Know Before Doing Business in Cuba." Entrepreneur. N.p., 30 Mar. 2016. Web. 01 May 2017. https://www.entrepreneur.com/article/273135.
[390] Kolarich, "17 Things."
[391] Id.

graduating over 4,000 IT engineers per year. Cuba's time zone and its geographical proximity are attractive bonuses for outsources.[392] In April 2017, Google's servers went live. This milestone comes four months after the company signed an agreement with Cuba's national telecom provider, ETECSA, to use its technology to make high-bandwidth activities faster. Another triumphant example of American business in Cuba is Airbnb. As of 3 October 2016, Airbnb had approximately 10,000 listings throughout the Republic of Cuba.

3.6C.2. Charcoal

So how does a company initiate business with Cuba. How does a company import items from Cuba? This author recommends doing it just like porcupines make love, "Very Carefully!" The first Cuban exports since the embargo went into effect over a half century ago arrived at Port Everglades in January 2017. Two containers of artisanal Cuban Marabú charcoal aboard K-Storm,[393] a Crowley Maritime ship docking at the Fort Lauderdale port.[394] The charcoal exports, which are produced by

---

[392] *Id*.

[393] The shipping line makes thrice-monthly trips from Port Everglades to Cuba's container port in Mariel and calls in Honduras and Guatemala before returning to the Fort Lauderdale port. Crowley mostly carries frozen chicken parts and foodstuffs to Cuba but it also handles small amounts of other legal exports to the island and was involved in shipping some of the equipment that the Rolling Stones used in their historic concert in Cuba in March 2016.

[394] An invasive woody species from Africa that is considered a nuisance on the island. In Cuba, Marabú has taken over wide swaths of idle agricultural land and strangled other plants. But it makes a hardwood charcoal that is winning

private worker-owned cooperatives, are legal under the support for the Cuban people policy initiatives instituted by the Obama administration allowing the importation of some products produced by independent Cuban entrepreneurs.[395]

By a stroke of luck, pure genius, or curious coincidence, Scott Gilbert chairs, Reneo Consulting, the parent company of Coabana Trading, which coordinated the charcoal deal with *CubaExport*, a Cuban government entity that develops trade opportunities by private Cuban cooperatives. Who is this Gilbert guy you ask? He is the same Scott Gilbert, the Washington D.C. lawyer who represented Alan Gross, the USAID subcontractor who was jailed as a spy by the Cuban government for five years.

"This is truly a momentous occasion," according to Gilbert. Stating when the deal for 40 tons of charcoal was announced earlier this year, U.S. patrons can purchase this product, as others have for many years.[396] Reflecting on the much larger significance, he further observed, "This marks the beginning of a new era of

---

acceptance as a fuel for pizza and bread ovens in Europe and the Middle East. It will be sold under the Fogo Charcoal brand by various U.S. retailers.
[395] Aquino, Jose, and Mimi Whitfield. "First Legal Cargo from Cuba in More Than Half-Century Arrives in the U.S." The Miami Herald. N.p., 2 Feb. 2017. Web. 28 Apr. 2017.
http://www.miamiherald.com/news/nationworld/world/americas/cuba/article128433209.html#storylink=cpy .
[396] *Id.*

trade between the United States and Cuba."

While this shipment was experimental, the looming implications for other importers to have regular shipments is huge. Jay Brickman, vice president of government services and Cuba service at Crowley, called the shipment "the first truly commercial shipment from a Cuban cooperative to a private U.S. business since the U.S.-Cuba trade embargo was imposed more than 50 years ago."[397] Once the proofs of principle are vetted, some analysts hopefully suggest this route for the future when large U.S. grocery chains and shopping clubs ship food, paint, and basic building materials to Cuba from the port.[398]

3.7. Cuba has limited capacity to absorb the American demand.

Irrespective of the increasing trade talk, the question remains, "Can Cuba handle the robustness of unfettered trade with the largest economy in the world?" American University Research Fellow at the Center for Latin American and Latino Studies, Fulton Armstrong argues —the main obstacle to expanding U.S.-Cuban economic ties is Cuba's own willingness and ability to conduct

---

[397] *Id.*
[398] *Id.*

trade, absorb investment, utilize information technology, and even accommodate tourists.[399] These limits risk putting a brake on the normalization of economic relations.

Mr. Armstrong sees big prospects in tourism, trade and investment, private sector, and agricultural sector, but concerned about the island's capacity to absorb expected development. First, the tourism industry is experienced and growing —at almost 4 million visitors per year— it could become an even more powerful producer income than the country can handle.[400] With major hotels at overcapacity, the hospitality business is seriously challenged to accommodate growth. Profitability potential is there, but if the U.S. Congress lifts the tourist travel ban, the industry would be overwhelmed.

Next, trade and foreign investment opportunities are available and could serve as powerful engines for growth and employment in Cuba. American political and business leaders' visits by Secretary Pritzker (October), U.S. Chamber President Donahue (May), trade delegations from New York, Texas, Arkansas, other

---

[399] Armstrong, Fulton. "Cuba's Limited Absorptive Capacity Will Slow Normalization." Cuba Initiative Policy Briefs. American University, 26 Oct. 2015. Web. 30 Apr. 2017. http://www.american.edu/clals/cuba_initiative-policy_briefs.cfm.
[400] Armstrong, "Cuba's Limited Absorptive Capacity"

states, and hundreds of U.S. importers, exporters, and investors underscore the eagerness of the U.S. private sector partner with Cubans. While investment seems promising, the question becomes will the government and the Cuban business community make investment safe and attractive.

Third, the private sector is booming. With over a million-people employed in this sector, private business is in the awkward position of being able to trade with the U.S. the most, but these small entrepreneurs lack reliable wholesale for essential supplies at home. The private sector is improved by a more supportive infrastructure, which could provide many more vital goods, services, and employment.[401]

Ultimately, Cuba has strong economic indicators, but it also has glaring capacity shortfalls. A variety of factors back holds Cuba's potential, including political caution; distorted dual currency; lack of streamline process for business approvals, and the over-burdened, secretive, and non-agile financial system.[402]

3.8. Forecast and Conclusion

Predictions and Conclusion

Forecasting President Trump's actions regarding Cuba is

---

[401] *Id.*
[402] *Id.*

risky and should be performed with great caution. In a New York Times opinion article, Jorge Dominiguez cites a Raul Castro joke that 'Fidel leads one [party] and I, the other.' Now, that Fidel Castro is dead; the ossified government he nurtured is vanishing as well.[403] In considering Trumps play on Cuba, first consider the cards he was dealt. Trump administration inherits agreements and policies reached by his three predecessors. Assuming after review, they serve both the interests of the Americans and Cubans, then "The Donald" may leave them in place or even move for further progress, if he's craving a policy victory. With headaches from Russia, ISIS, North Korea, China, and hemispheric problems, reversing or scaling back his Presidential-brethren' agreements, as Mr. Trump has threatened to do, will prove more difficult.[404]

The current bilateral cooperation supports remittances; hurricane and biodiversity protection; cancer research; infectious disease control, i.e., Zika epidemic; security matters; interdicting drug trafficking; unilateral aviation, just to name a few.[405]

As a prognostication, the United States and Cuban

---

[403] Domínguez, Jorge I. "Opinion | Can Donald Trump and Raúl Castro Make a Good Deal?" The New York Times. The New York Times, 10 Jan. 2017. Web. 28 Apr. 2017. https://www.nytimes.com/2017/01/10/opinion/can-donald-trump-and-raul-castro-make-a-good-deal.html.
[404] Id.
[405] Id.

leadership have three options in moving forward: 1) Do more; 2) Do less; or 3) Do nothing! Of course, that is not an earth-shattering prediction of what is on the horizon and international relations are extremely complicated, the choices are just that simple.

With the codification of the main elements of the Helms-Burton Cuban embargo, the regional, hemispheric, and international community's frustration, and the Obama administration's nearly unfettered easing, President Trump is in a virtual "Check" position. First, the Helms-Burton LIBERTAD act and other embargo legal framework dictate a rigorous compliance with some incredibly stiff penalties, which means Mr. Trump's potential policies are restricted from being more aggressive in the thawing of relations than his predecessor absent a Congressional lifting of sanctions.

Next, Mr. Trump's relations with the regional, hemispheric, and international community and standing is jeopardized with a doing less. The Organization of American States ("OAS") has given full throated support for Cuba and any attempt to re-exclude the island from a seat at the table will likely trigger protest and non-participatory attitudes by our Latin American neighbors. Not continuing to suspend certain sections of Title III and IV economic embargo like each President since the embargo's inception, would provide strong indicia of his intentions to the international community. This inaction would automatically prompt the more aggressive extraterritorial provisions of Helms-Burton.

The U.N. General Assembly has passed a resolution calling for the "necessity of ending the economic, commercial, and financial embargo imposed by the United States of America against Cuba" every year since its enactment. The international community has expressed strong disapproval of these types of extraterritorial sanctions measures, and likely to actuate the anti-blocking countermeasures of many of the U.S. allies mainly U.K., E.U., Canada, and Mexico.

Additionally, Mr. Trump is hamstrung by former President Obama's setting optimistic expectations because any move that he makes could prove catastrophic. If he disengages, he potentially ostracizes and isolates the U.S. regionally and abroad. If he engages further, he upsets the ever-dwindling minority of Cuba hawks that irrationally desire regime change in a nation they don't live in. With the full plate and onslaught of daily distractors, this researcher predicts President Trump will punt by continuing the 6-month suspension of Titles III and IV until a Castro family is no longer in office. Additionally, Mr. Trump will maintain the status quo of the Obama easing measures for further impact study of American interest.

Finally, Mr. Trump will implore his National Security Team to slowly vet Cuba in order to validate trust. The feel good moment of reengagement must not risk American lives. Diplomatic tensions between Cuba and the US remain high after the appearance of mysterious "acoustic attacks." As the author has worked in multiple U.S. embassies, the President and the Ambassadors must keep the staff and visiting Americans safe. According to the State Department dozens of U.S. Embassy at Havana have had their health affected. President Trump has to find this unacceptable and he must work with the Cuban leadership to fully investigate this unacceptable posture toward American embassy personnel whether the attacks where Cuban grown or otherwise.

Now, what will Castro do? That is much more challenging but the choices are somehow very similar to Trump's limitations. In 2018, Raul Castro stepped down from the presidency and allow the newly-elected National Assembly to choose a new leader. But what if chooses to stay on longer as the leader of the Communist Party?[406] What if the assembly implores him to stay?

Notwithstanding that option, outside and domestic

---

[406] First Secretary of the Central Committee of the Communist Party of Cuba

pundits speculate President Miguel Diaz-Canel as his successor. Diaz-Canel is a 58-year-old career Communist Party official whose low-key nature leaves many Cubans unconvinced of his ability to be the first top Cuban leader from outside the Castro family since 1959.

After speaking to many Cuban citizens, young and old, whether *procastristas* or *anticastristas*, A.D. Winters gathers that many Cubanos are weary of Diaz-Canel leadership and just want to wait and see. The "unscientific microsampling" leads the author to believe that many Cubans prefer their next leader to be cut from the same revolutionary cloth as the Castros. Off the record, one Cubana lawyer and part-time tour guide, advised that she doesn't get the impression of strength from Diaz-Canel. While at a private *Santeria*[407] ceremony, an Afro-Cubano told A.D. Winters that he fears Diaz-Canel's somewhat laid back mannerism will encourage various factions to divide Cuba. In another instance, while researching the public bus system, a group of Cuban gentlemen in their mid-50s opined that Diaz-Canel strikes them as a transitory leader not a ten-plus year leader.

---

[407] Santeria (Way of the Saints or worship of saints) is an Afro-Caribbean religion based on Yoruba beliefs and traditions, with some Roman Catholic elements added. The religion is also known as *La Regla Lucumi* and *the Rule of Osha*. Santeria is a syncretic religion that grew out of the slave trade in Cuba. The enslaved Yoruba people were pretty ingenious to develop this under the nose of their Christian captors.

Considering this all but settled, new conjecture is brewing since Raul's daughter made a statement in May 2017? According to a May 3rd Michael Weissenstein's associated press article, in response to a succession process inquiry, Mariela Castro said: "Sometimes you're going in one direction and suddenly you look over here and go, 'Wow, how interesting, I hadn't focused on this person. There are always surprises," she concluded. Internationally known for her gay-rights advocacy, Mariela is also member of Cuba's National Assembly. She has long been one of Cuba's most outspoken public figures, and her statements are largely seen as congruent with her father's. Additionally, as most Cubans and the international community would remind Americans, don't inaugurate a person before they are officially elected.

Thus, by the lack of concreteness of Raul stepping down as First Secretary until it happens, and the recent speculation created by Mariel's statement, this author forecasts Cuba will continue lobbying for international and regional unanimity for lifting of the U.S. "blockade." Likewise, Cuba will incrementally improve infrastructure no matter how de minimus to attract substantial foreign investment. With the increasing cost of communism "freebies" and ever-growing private sector, the island will drift closer toward its version of a mixed market economy. As outside influences increase through technology, the societal expectations will drive new norms.

Conclusion

In closing, the Cuban people will determine their destiny more, and the government will control it less. As Americans, we will just be along for the classic American car ride to *La Floridita* to enjoy mojitos, daiquiris, and of course, the *Cuba Libres*.

CHAPTER 4: QUICK GUIDE TO VISITING CUBA

Before going to Cuba, develop a thorough plan and coordinate with a reputable company that will ensure that your reasoning pursuant to one of the 12 legitimate OFAC ordained reasoning for an American traveling to Cuba fulfills your goal and provides a pleasant experience.

From the time, you exit to the aircraft, ferry, or cruise ship, this is a quick-reference of places to see and things to do enhance your educational experience, religious experience, or strengthen your support for the Cuban people.

4.0 Look Before You Leap to the Pearl of the Caribbean

When traveling to Cuba, develop a complete plan in order to maximize the experience. The Pearl of the Caribbean is beautiful and intriguing. The people are amazing and the culture is fascinating. If you plan the travel correctly, then you can discover the heart and soul of the Cuban society.

A preferred trip would take seven days or whatever your itinerary dictates. After earning his Juris Doctorate at Southern University Law Center in Baton Rouge and serving as Assistant Attorney General with the Louisiana Department of Justice, coupled with his over two decades of military service abroad (working in multiple U.S. Embassies), he took a keen interest in international affairs. While the author earned his two Masters of Laws ('LL.M.') at the University of Houston Law Center: (1) International Law and (2) Energy, Environmental, and Natural Resources Law, the author focused primarily on the future of Cuba mainly with respects to its foreign and business relations with the U.S.

The following checklist was based on the author's first itinerary while cross-enrolled in a law class in Havana with the Mississippi College of Law in conjunction with the Cuba Explorer and Universidad de Habana. The class focused on candid peer-to-peer examination of the Cuban legal system and exploration of Cuban culture.

Like all first trips to a foreign land, a traveler should have an escort. Cuba Explorer provided an expert English-speaking Cuban guide versed in law, history, and culture. For transportation, the tour used a luxury tour coach and dedicated chauffer. The tour included island-side in and out airport transfers. The tour included some of the meals: All breakfasts were included. Many lunches and dinners were provided as detailed below in the class tuition and fees. This was unnecessarily pricey versus the local market prices, but considering that since we didn't just dine at the tourist havens, the price was ultimately worth it. We traveled deeper into the greater Havana region to explore farms, *paladares*, cantinas, and *fincas* and ended up experiencing why many food critics consider the Cuban food market to be on fire or *en fueugo*.

4.1 On Day 1 – Debarkation into Cuba

- Arrival at Havana's José Martí International Airport. Collect your bags and go through customs.
- You're welcomed at the airport lobby by your Cuba Education Tours (INSERT YOUR COMPANY'S) guide (EXCHANGE USDs for CUCs a limited amount as you may get a better rate in the HAVANA at the Bank or your lodging option)

- Ignore the Hustle and Bustle and go straight for professional bus chauffeur (***INSERT YOUR TRANSPORTATION SOLUTION***). Plenty of Taxes at the Airport (Generally $25-35 CUC for a taxi and luggage to Havana. Have your address in hand.
- Your guide will direct you to a bank or exchange bureau (CADECA) to purchase more Cuban Convertible Pesos (CUC). Cuba has a dual currency system that is not traded on the international currency market.
- Schedule free time after check in to settle in and rest up at your lodging.
- Discover your surroundings and find your bottled water and pantry items for your room.

4.2 On Day 2: - *Exploring the city of Havana and its rich history*

- In the morning visit to the *Maqueta de La Habana Vieja*. It's a 1:500 scale model of Old Havana, which is complete with an authentic soundtrack meant to replicate a day in the life of the city. It's incredibly detailed and provides an excellent way of geographically acquainting yourself with the city's historical core. The model is used for social development and planning.

- Next take a walking tour of Old Havana, a UNESCO World Heritage Site. Here, experience the city by visiting four of the five historic plazas (religious in nature having a church in these four squares) that make Havana unique in the western hemisphere. It contains the largest collection of remaining colonial-era architecture. This tour is best led by a Cuban Educational Tours' guide.

- First up, the **Cathedral Square** regarded as the most beautiful and private 18th century colonial plaza on the island. Named after the masterpiece of Cuban baroque architecture: the *Catedral de San Cristóbal de la Habana* built by the Jesuit order.
- Second, visit the **Square of Arms**, an ancient military parade ground for Spanish soldiers, surrounded by impressive buildings such as: * *Palacio de los Capitanes Generales*, former seat of colonial government. Today the building houses the Museum of the City of Havana.
- Next, continue onto San Francisco Square, which is one of the oldest plazas in the historical quarter. The square is named after magnificent *Iglesia y Monasterio de San Francisco de Asís* dating from the 16th century. The basilica is a striking example of Cuba baroque architecture.
- And finally travel to *Plaza Vieja*, the only civic square of colonial times. Absent are churches and government buildings, and is in contrast surrounded by opulent aristocratic 17th century

residences. We'll visit an important center for the visual arts.

After all of the walking, learning, and touring, you are no doubt famished. This author recommends lunch at *La Moneda Cubana,* private restaurant where you'll enjoy traditional Cuban dishes. There are plenty of choices for the budget conscience, so this is definitely not your only choice. After refueling, then back to the cultural awareness.

- Next up, visit the *Centro Cultural Antiguos Almacenes de Depósito San José*. This marvelous restoration of an old dock warehouse has resulted in a gigantic market exhibiting the wares of hundreds of Cuban artists and craftspersons. (UPDATE: As of July 2018, the market is closed due to a fire).
- In continuation artisan exploration, then visit *Callejón de Hamel* (Hamel Alley) to see the artwork of famed Afro-Cuban Artist Salvador González, known for paintings, murals, and sculptors. His work is best described as a mix of surrealism, cubism, and abstract art.

At this point, it is best to take an afternoon rest and prepare for an evening of exploration and awareness:

- To start the evening, try dinner at *Restaurant El Patio*, or your preference.

- Evening highlight: Witness a very dramatic ceremony – *El Cañonazo* – the firing of the *9PM Cannon* at the Fortress of San Carlos de la Cabaña. This enchanting colonial reenactment dates back to 1519 when the city of Havana was enclosed by a tall thick rock wall to ward off attacks from pirates and the English. The cannon firing signaled the closing of the city gates for the night. If you were outside at the time, you were in "*Vedado*" or the forbidden zone. Today, *Vedado* is an important cultural hub and beautiful section of modern Havana.

4.3 On Day 3: – Ernest Hemingway's house

- Volunteer at a pre-coordinated cleanup or take in an art class.
- For lunch try *El Ajiaco*, which serves Cuban creole dishes at private restaurant.
- Visit *Cojímar*, small fishing village one of Hemingway's favorites places in Cuba.
- Then visit *Finca Vigía* [Lookout Farm] where North America's literary giant Ernest Hemingway spent twenty-one of his most important and productive years penning building blocks of English literature. Claimed by both the United States and Cuba as their son, it was Hemingway himself who declared the island his true home. The house has been preserved just as it was when Hemingway lived there. You'll see his personal objects, thousands of books and photographs, as

well as some "trophies" bagged on his frequent safaris.
- Rest for the evening and take in one of Havana's Jazz Café's

4.4 On Day 4: – Community services, dance

- Breakfast in hotel
- Take in a Cuban Cultural class from 8:30 am to 11:30 am
- Take out some time for a very special lunch. On this day, get reservations at *El Santo Ángel* restaurant, which is a beautiful colonial mansion.

As a humanitarian health project, visit the *Convento de Nuestra Señora de Belén* [Convent of Our Lady of Belén], in Old Havana. Construction on the Convent was begun in 1712. It was expanded and remodeled several times over the centuries. Finally abandoned in 1925, it fell into grave disrepair. In 1991 restoration began and continues with amazing results. Today the Office of the Historian, local Public Health authorities and the Order of the Sisters of Charity jointly manage the Belén Convent. It is home to fifty elderly people and provides physiotherapy and ophthalmological services to many more elderly in the community. Other activities include exercise classes, board games, cognitive rehabilitation, films and crafts workshops.

- To continue with the cultural people to people engagement, visit **Dance Group Retazos**:

Retazos is a center for the promotion of dance under the Ministry of Culture of Cuba and the Office of the Historian of Old Havana. It is run by Isabel Bustos, a former professor at the National School of Modern Dance and the University of the Arts in Cuba.

- Watch a performance by *Grupo Retazos*.
- Recommended evening entertainment: *Jazz Club La Zorra y el Cuervo*

4.5 On Day 5: – *Education and history*

A fantastic place to visit is the Community Project *Muraleando*. Muraleando is an art center in Havana founded by Manuel Diaz Baldrich. The center was inspired by the children of the community. Music, dance, sculpting, painting and other fine arts are all part of the

project which transforms children's lives. Many of them come from low income families or have behavioral problems, art is their outlet.

- *Muraleando* has a great lunch menu.

After leaving *Muraleando,* visit The Museum of the Revolution. The Museum of the Revolution is a museum located in the Old Havana section of Havana. The museum is housed in what was the Presidential Palace of all Cuban presidents from Mario García Menocal to Fulgencio Batista. It became the Museum of the Revolution during the years following the Cuban revolution.

- **EVENING ENTERTAINMENT SUGGESTION:** Casa de la Música de Centro Habana, one of the best settings to listen to great traditional music. Dance with Cubans and foreign visitors.

4.6 Day 6 – *Community services*

- Visit *Proyecto El Divino*, a model farm with two community projects supported by proceeds from its amazing restaurant.

El Divino serves lunch to some 20 local elders who also enjoy a place of entertainment, socialization and recreation. A great place to play dominos with elder Cuban. Watch out, these are experts. Together for several hours a day from Tuesday to Sunday, they play games and engage with other groups of elders. Another project is a circle of interest called "La Rosa Blanca" that welcomes about 20 community kids aged 8 to 11 years. They take classes on ecology, environment, care and protection of land, and link their studies to Cuban culture and manners: to be men and women of good will in the not too distant future. This incredible Cuban project donates a portion of its meager proceeds to similar projects in Latin American, and holds a certificate of excellence from Trip Advisor.

- Lunch at *El Divino* is amazing.

Next, visit *Santa María* beach, which is a lush white sands beach with the warm blue waters.

• Entertainment Recommendation: SPECIAL *"¡Noche De Fiesta Cubana!"* party with live music at Club Karachi.

4.7 Day 7: – Arts, Domestic and International Law in Cuba

Visit and travel to *Jaimanitas*. Here, you will find *José Fúster*, one of Cuba's most important ceramists and painters at his whimsical studio in, just outside of Havana. In the afternoon, coordinate a meeting with representatives of the *Bufete de Servicios Legales Especializados* – ONBC (National Organization of Collective Law). The national organization has similarities to the American Bar Association. It began in 1965 with the aim of achieving a representation of a social nature with equal opportunities for all, in the areas of Criminal Law, Civil, Administrative and Labor.

Bufete Collective Growth

Today this collective has grown to a network of 252 law offices across the country, providing free legal services to over 65,000 Cubans annually. The theme of the encounter was threefold. The Cuban lawyers provided a presentation followed by:

- Q&A and wide-open discussion.
- The Structure and Role of Specialized Cuban Law Collectives.
- The Role of the Cuban Lawyer Today.

CHAPTER 5: PHOTO COLLAGE FROM THE PEARL OF THE CARRIBEAN

The following is a quick photo collage of great locations throughout Havana and the surrounding area.

AMERICAN PO' BOY EN CUBA

A.D. Winters, Esq. LLM[2]

AMERICAN PO' BOY EN CUBA

A.D. Winters, Esq. LLM²

AMERICAN PO' BOY EN CUBA

A.D. Winters, Esq. LLM[2]

AMERICAN PO' BOY

EN CUBA

A.D. WINTERS, ESQ. LLM[2]

www.ingramcontent.com/pod-product-compliance
Lightning Source LLC
Chambersburg PA
CBHW032022230426
43671CB00005B/167